MOUNTAINEERING:

A Bibliography of Books
in English to 1974

compiled by

CHESS KRAWCZYK

The Scarecrow Press, Inc.

Metuchen, N.J.   1977

Library of Congress Cataloging in Publication Data

Krawczyk, Chess, 1947-
  Mountaineering.

  Includes indexes.
  1. Mountaineering—Bibliography. I. Title.
Z6016.M7K72 [GV200] 016.7965'22 76-45415
ISBN 0-8108-0979-6

ii

To the women
who drove me to the mountains.

THE WANDERER

"And whatever may still overtake me as fate and experience--a wandering will be therein, and a mountain climbing; in the end one experienced only oneself. "

... Thus Spake Zarathustra.

TABLE OF CONTENTS

INTRODUCTION

This bibliography combines two interests: librarianship and mountaineering. As a rock climber, many of my
techniques were learned from the books listed herein, these
ideas being put into practice on the rock face. The amount
of time available to go climbing is severely limited for many
people with routine obligations of home and work and this
leads to the dominant interest of seeking satisfaction by vi-
cariously sharing the exploits of others. This enjoyment is
contagious to non-climbers and has resulted in the growth of
so called "armchair" mountaineers, and has stimulated the
number of books written and their popularity among the general reading public.

As with other specialized subjects, the amount of literature soon grows to the stage that a review or cumulation
of contents becomes necessary. Thus reading lists are produced, shelflists of contents of specialized collections are
published and finally attempts are made to compile a definitive bibliography. This is such an attempt which hopes to
fill part of this gap in the literature of mountaineering.

The origins of this book lie in the shelflist of a public
library, supplemented by the bibliographies contained in many
of that library's books. It was originally intended as a personal reading list but grew out of proportion. The inspiration
and idea of compiling a bibliography from this base came as
a result of acquiring a copy of Janet Adam Smith's Mountaineering; from this work several abstracts have been drawn,
with the kind permission of the National Book League.

Once started, standard bibliographic tools were used to
expand and locate further information; in particular they pro-
vided a standard of bibliographic description usually lacking
in other works. As a result of searches, previously published
mountaineering bibliographies were noted, acquired and incor-
porated into this work. The existence of bibliographies of
mountaineering and rock-climbing collections prompted a suc-

cessful canvass of likely organizations, which, without ex-
ception, were very cooperative. This resulted in a working
collection of titles on cards which often required verification.
This proved to be the hardest task, as it required the actual
search for those titles in various libraries in order that they
could be reviewed. The reviews were supplemented by published reviews wherever possible.

The above research produced a wealth of data that required processing to avoid duplication, the exclusion of irrele-
vant works (a subjective process), resolving contradictions like
the spelling of an author's name (or even determining who the
author is), exclusion of foreign-language books, conversion into a standard bibliographic format, and finally, supplementing
with information from other sources.

It soon became apparent that the task could not be totally completed: as the size of the bibliography increased, the
amount of effort required to add to it increased corresponding-
ly. The law of greatly diminishing returns turned out in
practice to limit this bibliography to its present size. When
the last few existing bibliographies were being examined, fewer and fewer new items were found. The same law of diminishing returns applied to the verification of incomplete data,
namely, to locate an item in one of the national bibliographies
took more and more effort as the work became more obscure.
This is why several entries are incomplete in the text. The
problem of compiling a work of this nature from the semi-
isolation of Australia without direct access to large libraries
is significant.

The Scope

When planning the extent of this bibliography, several
limitations became evident early in consideration. Firstly,
foreign language books were excluded because of the absence
of reference material within easy access. Secondly, guide
books to particular areas were excluded for several reasons,
namely, their limited geographic value, the existence of an
excellent bibliography for Britain by G. Bridge, their dated-
ness, and the belief that climbers interested in particular
areas can locate such guides by reference to local organizations. Lastly, the most difficult task was to define mountaineering and rock climbing, and to exclude books which lay
outside these limits. The definition was relaxed for early
published books that cover the period when travellers scram-
bled up mountains and called this mountaineering. The defini-

tion therefore includes books on rock, snow and ice climbing, with the emphasis on climbing; marginal interest topics, such as equipment, techniques, rescue, and exploration; and biographies of noted climbers. Where books noted were of doubtful interest they were included. Any additions or amendments would be gratefully received by the author.

Format

This bibliography is arranged into author, title and subject sequences; the author entry contains the complete information pertaining to a book, while the title and subject entries refer back to the serial number of the author entry. The title index consists of abbreviated title entries for all books in the author sequence. The subject index groups the books by subject categories.

The actual layout of the author entry is based on the International Standard Bibliographic Description for Monographs (I. S. B. D. (M)). In practice, this results in the following layout:

1234 SURNAME, Forename Forename
      Title: subtitle or parallel titles / by an author, in-
      cluding joint authors. - Edition statement. - Place
      of publication: publisher, date. - collation.

The initial strangeness of the punctuation conventions should be easily overcome with familiarity; namely, ". -" signifies a separation between parts of the bibliographic description, while the "/" signifies the separation of full title from the authorship statement. The adoption in this bibliography of I. S. B. D. (M) was prompted by the use of this convention in national bibliographies and the projected adoption by most libraries in the future.

Following the bibliographic description there are reviews of many of the books. These are identified by abbreviations relating to their source. These abbreviations are:

BBN	British Book News
BRD	Book Review Digest
Campbell	A bibliography of mountains and mountaineering in Africa
Dawson's	secondhand catalogs from Dawson's Bookshop, Los Angeles

Ed.   personally reviewed books

GCPL   Glasgow Corporation Public Library

NBL   National Book League (i. e. , Janet Adam
                     Smith)

NUC. LC   National Union Catalog, Library of Con-
                     gress

RHB   Robert Hicks Bates

Speleobooks   Speleobooks catalog

Yakushi   Bibliography on Everest

Summary

To one examining the books listed in this bibliography, several definite trends become apparent. First, in historical perspective, the early books are by travelers who were drawn to the mountains and indulged in scrambles to minor summits or peaks. Mountaineering as such may be seen as having its origins in the desire to reach previously unattainable peaks; thus Horace Benedict de Saussure in his preoccupation with Mont Blanc foreshadows the growth of mountaineering. With the publicity following on from the conquest of Mont Blanc by such people as Albert Smith, there starts a stream of litera- ture by persons who climb a mountain and immediately after write a record of their exploits. Some of this has literary merit, most was of interest in its period, the rest is of in- terest only to historians. What this period did discover was that the reading public was demanding more of these adventure stories, even though only a small minority were inspired to try the sport. At the same time notable individuals were be- coming devoted to this recreation as a sport; from the Brit- ish viewpoint expressed within these books, one feels that the English created this sport and it was then taken up by the rest of Europe.

The interest in mountains, once it was realized that man could reach the tops and survive (!), led to travels to far distant lands and the spirit of competition to conquer the unclimbed peaks. The character of the pioneers is an in- triguing sidelight; in the main they were professional or academically minded, well-to-do gentlemen with plenty of spare time and few financial restraints. This background soon defined the highest peaks to be climbed, with Mount Everest as the ultimate goal. Simultaneously, rock climbing

as a sport was born in the British Isles, firstly as a practice
for the serious European climbing; then in its own right.
Thus training manuals were written, local climbs and climbers were noted in print, and, most importantly, numerous
persons and not only armchair mountaineers became active.
The same period saw the continual publication of mountaineering books to keep the public enthralled.

Mount Everest and the other 8000-meter peaks domi-
nated the public's attention from the early 1930's, while at
home, technical training manuals and new routes in the Alps
were avidly read and discussed by the climbers.   The attempts, reconnaissance and final success have been a steady
source of interest up to the present day.   As the major peaks
fell, lesser peaks claimed the attention of the competition-
minded climbers and the reading public.

Once exploration lapsed as a motive, mountaineering
became identified with technical rock climbing; new climbers
repeated old routes with variations, found new ascent routes
up previously climbed peaks.   The question of why men and
women climb mountains is contained in the books listed in
this bibliography; the question of why people read such books
has never been asked.

The development of this branch of literature is conventional to the extent that out-of-print books have been re-
issued, sometimes many times in various editions, some authors making their fame by abridging well-known works or
editing anthologies.   In fact, as the literature grew many
books were written on the basis of previous works with no
new primary sources.   The last stage of this process is the
appearance of books about the books--that is, bibliographies;
the present work is partly a bibliography of these bibliographies.

There are a few critical points that need to be made
in retrospect.   First, quite a few of the books are in the
style of the cheaper novels; they are potboilers, or attempts
to capitalize on a ready market without having anything new
to say.   Also, a person who writes several books on the
basis of one or a few experiences usually has very little to
say.   As far as adventure books are concerned, as Robert
Bates notes, the literary ability or literacy of some writers
is at a low level.   In some cases, there is a lack of orig-
inality; for example, two books claim for a title the meta-
phor, Tiger of the Snow: one refers to A. F. Mummery,
the other to Tenzing.   The number of books with similar titles

xi

indicate that many authors are not aware of the literature to which they are contributing. In the matter of climbing manuals, new editions of outdated works are still being republished and new manuals vastly inferior to existing works still appear from time to time.

As a bibliography, this book should make interested persons aware of what has been printed through 1973. This may create a desire to read or acquire the original works; unfortunately, this is a difficult task. Most public libraries have representative collections; some of sufficient size to justify printing a selected reading list; others may hold special collections or even be specially devoted to such collections. Secondhand bookshops usually have a quick turnover of any book that finds its way onto their shelves. Occasionally, a private collection is offered for sale or auction.

ACKNOWLEDGMENTS

On a personal note I would like to express my gratitude to the City of Greater Wollongong Public Library, where I started this work, and the University of Wollongong Library where it was completed. I want to thank those of my colleagues who encouraged my efforts and assisted in many ways. Most importantly, I wish to thank Mrs. A. Genero and Mrs. K. Cooper for typing up my cards; and Mrs. J. Gilroy for the unenviable task of preparing the manuscript.

C. J. K.

THE BIBLIOGRAPHY

Herein are found the full entries for books, in a
listing arranged by author and serially numbered.
Cross references from persons as subjects and
from joint or co-authors to main entry authors
are in this sequence.

01 ABBAT, Richard
       The ascent of Scawfell Pike / by Richard Abbat. -
    London: 1851.

    ABNEY, W. de W.   see   CUNNINGHAM, Carus Dunlop
         (235)

02 ABRAHAM, Ashley Perry
       Rock climbing in Skye / by Ashley Perry Abraham. -
    London: Longmans, 1908. - 330 p. : 30 ill., 9 diagr.,
    map.
         See also ABRAHAM, George Dixon (09)

03 ABRAHAM, George Dixon
       British mountain climbs ... with 18 illustrations and
    21 outline drawings / by George Abraham. - 6th ed. -
    London: Mills and Doon, 1948. - 448 p.
       First pub. 1909.

04 _____.
       The complete mountaineer / by George D. Abraham. -
    3rd ed. - London: Methuen, 1923. - 495 p. : 75 ill.
       First pub. 1907.

05 _____.
       First steps to climbing / by George Abraham. - Lon-
    don: Mills and Boon, 1923. - 126 p. : 24 ill.
       "A very practical guide to the sport of rockclimbing
    for beginners, lists equipment, snow and icecraft plus a
    list of famous British climbing centres. " BRD.

06 _____ .
Modern mountaineering/ by George Abraham. - 3rd
ed. - London: Methuen, 1949. - 198 p.
"Two brothers, professional photographers and inde-
fatigable rock climbers, with first ascents and unrivalled
experience of their time." NBL.

07 _____ .
Mountain adventure at home and abroad/ by George
Abraham. - London: Methuen, 1910. - 308 p.: 26 ill.

08 _____ .
On Alpine heights and British crags/ by George
Abraham. - Boston: Houghton Mifflin, 1916. - 307 p.:
24 ill.

09 _____ .
Rock climbing in North Wales/ by George and Ashley Abraham. - Keswick: G. P. Abraham, 1906. - 394
p.: 30 plates.

10 _____ .
Swiss mountain climbs/ by George Abraham. - London: Mills and Boon, 1911. - 432 p.: 24 ill., 22 outline
drawings.

11 ACADEMIC ALPINE CLUB OF KYOTO
Japanese Chogolisa expedition/ by the Academic Alpine Club of Kyoto. - Kyoto, Japan: the Club, 1959.

12 ADAMS, William Henry Davenport
Alpine adventure: or narratives of travel and research in the Alps/ by the author of "The Mediterranean
illustrated". - London: Nelson, 1878. - 239 p.: ill.

13 _____ .
Alpine climbing/ by William H. D. Adams. - London: 1881.

14 ADIRONDACK FORTY-SIXERS
New York: Private, 1958. - 147 p.: ill., Printing
a limited edition of 400 copies.
"The Adirondack Forty-sixers consist of members of
the Adirondack Mountain Club who have climbed all forty-
six peaks of the Adirondack High Peak region." Dawson's.

15 AHLUWALIN, H. P. S.
Higher than Everest: Memoirs of a mountaineer/

by H. P. S. Ahluwalin, with a foreword by Indira Gandhi.
- Delhi: Vikas, 1973. - 188 p. : 21 1/2 cm.

15a AIREY, A. F.
Irish hill days/ by A. F. Airey. - Manchester:
1930's.

15b AITKEN, S.
Among the Alps: a narrative of personal experience/
by S. Aitken. - [S. L.]: the Author, 1900. - ill.
Privately pub.

16 ALACK, Frank
Guide aspiring/ by F. Alack. - Ed. by J. Halket
Millar. - Auckland: Oswald-Sealy, 1963. - 229 p. : ill.

17 ALEXANDER, Sir Henry
The Cairngorms/ by Sir H. Alexander. - 4th ed. /
rev. by A. Watson and others. - Edinburgh: Scottish
Mountaineering Trust.

18 ALPINE CLUB, London
The Alpine annual 1950/ adapted from the 1949 num-
bers of the Alpine Journal. - London: Dent, 1950.

19
The Alpine journal: a record of mountain adventure
and scientific observation. - London: The Alpine Club,
dist. by West Col Productions.

20
Equipment for mountaineers. - London: 1892.
(New author) ALPINE CLUB - Special Committee on
Equipment for mountaineers. Provisional Report/ Lon-
don: 1891.
See also COCKBURN, Henry (100)

21 ALPINE CLUB OF CANADA, Montreal Section
Mountaineering around Montreal: an unofficial and
preliminary attempt at a local guidebook for rockclimbing, mountain walking and camping (plus ski touring and
canoeing)/ by the Montreal Section, Alpine Club of Canada, and Le Club de montagne Canadien. - Point Claire,
Que. : the Club, 1964. - 351. : maps, 22cm.

22 AMERICAN ALPINE CLUB
Accidents in American mountaineering: annual reports of the Safety Committee of the American Alpine

Club. - New York: American Alpine Club, 1947.

23 AMERY, Rt. Hon. Leopold Charles Maurice Stennett
    Days of fresh air: being reminiscences of outdoor
    life/ by L. C. M. S. Amery. - London: Jarrolds,
    1939. - 320 p. : plates.

24 _____.
        In the rain and the sun: a sequel to "Days of Fresh
    air"/ by L. C. M. S. Amery. - London: Hutchinson,
    1946. - 251 p. : plates

25 ANDEREGG, Melchoir
        In memoriam: Melchoir Anderegg. - Reprinted from
    the Alpine Journal, Vol. 29, 1959. p. 56-73.

26 ANDERSON, Eustace
        Chamouni and Mont Blanc: a visit to the valley and
    an ascent of the mountain in the autumn of 1855/ by Eu-
    stace Anderson. - London: James Cornish, 1856. -
    113 p.

27 ANDERSON, John Richard Lane
        The Ulysses factor: the exploring instinct in man/
    by John Anderson. - London: Hodder & Stoughton,
    1970. - 352 p. : 7 plates, 1 ill. , ports.
        His own theory as to why men risk difficult condi-
    tions. Includes chapters on Shipton, Tilman and Herzog.
    Ed.

28 ANDERSON, Michael
        Mittel Switzerland/ comp. by Michael Anderson. -
    Reading: West Col Productions, 1974. - 51 p. : ill. ,
    maps, 18cm. (Pilot Alpine guides)

29 ANDERSON, Mona
        River rules my life/ by Mona Anderson. - Welling-
    ton: Reed, 1963. - 212 p. : 24 plates, map.
        "Mt. Olgidus, New Zealand. "

    ANDREWS, A. W. see J. M. A. THOMSON (976)

30 ARNOLD-BROWN, Adam
        Unfolding character: the impact of Gordonstoun/ by
    Adam Arnold-Brown. - London: Routledge & Kegan Paul,
    1962. - 246 p. : plates, tables, 21 1/2 cm.

31 ARUNDALE, George S.
Mount Everest: its spiritual attainment/ by George
S. Arundale. - Wheaton, Ill. : Theosophical Press,
1933. - 197 p.

32 ASCENT TO THE SUMMIT OF COCK'S COMB MOUNTAIN

ASHCROFT, Jack see RUSSELL, Jean (828)

ASHENDEN (pseud.) see NOWILL, Sidney Edward Pyn
(702)

ASHLEY; Mildred P. see FARQUHAR, Francis Peloubet
(305)

33 ASSOCIATION OF BRITISH MEMBERS OF THE SWISS AL-
PINE CLUB
Mountaineering handbook: a complete and practical
guide for beginner or expert. - London: the Association,
1960. - 168 p. : ill.

34 ATKINS, Henry Martin
Ascent to the summit of Mont Blanc on the 22nd and
23rd of August, 1837/ by Henry Martin Atkins. - London:
the Author, 1838. - 49p. : plates.
Intro. signed J. G. Children.

35 AUDEN, Wystan Hugh
The ascent of F6/ by W. H. Auden and Christopher
Isherwood. - New York: 1937.
"A not impressive satire in verse. " RHB.

36 AULDJO, John
Narrative of an ascent to the summit of Mont Blanc
on the 8th and 9th of August, 1827/ by John Auldjo. -
London: Longmans, 1828. - ix, 12p. : maps,
plates.
"The author's ascent won him a gold medal from one
king and a diamond ring from another. Writes with dig-
nity, courage and determination ... without any kindred
feeling for the mountains. " RHB.

37 AUSTIN, Cecil K.
On mountain climbing for professional men/ by Cecil
K. Austin. - Boston: 1907.

38 AUSTRALIAN ANDEAN EXPEDITION, 1969
        The Australian Andean expedition, 1969. - Wahroonga,
    N. S. W. :   the Secretary AAE, 1969. - 32p. : ill. , diagr. ,
    map.
        A well illustrated pamphlet, with good photography;
    used to recoup some of the expenses of the expedition.
    Ed.

39 AZEMA, Marc Antonin
        The conquest of Fitzroy / by M. A. Azema. - trans.
    from the French by Katherine Chorley and Nea Morin. -
    London: Deutsch, 1957. - 237p. : 12 plates, maps.
        Orig. pub. as La Conquête du Fitz Roy. Paris,
    Flammarion, 1954.

40 BADDELEY, Mountford John B.
        The Peak district / by M. J. B. Baddeley. - 11th
    ed. , rewritten. - London: Ward, Lock, 1930's. - 152
    p. : ill.

41 BAEDEKER, Karl
        Eastern Alps: including the Bavarian Highlands, the
    Tyrol, Salzkammergut, Styria and Corinthia / by Karl
    Baedeker. - 4th ed. , remodeled and augmented. - Lei-
    pzig: Karl Baedeker, 1879. - xxx, 438 p.

42 BAGLEY, Arthur L.
        Walks and scrambles in the highlands / by A. L.
    Bagley. - London: Skeffington & Sons, 1914. - 204 p.

    BAILLIE-GROHMAN, W. A. see GROHMAN, William
        Adolph Baillie (388)

43 BAKER, Ernest Albert
        The British highlands with rope and rucksack / by
    E. A. Baker. - London: Witherby, 1933. - 236 p. : ill.
        First pub. as The highlands with rope and rucksack,
    1923.

44   _____.
        Moors, crags and caves of the high peak / by Ernest
    A. Baker. - Manchester: Heywood, 1903. - 207 p. : ill.

45   _____.
        On foot in the highlands / E. A. Baker. - London:
    Maclehose, 1932. - 199 p. : plates

46 _____ .
        The voice of the mountains: an anthology/ ed. by
E. A. Baker and Francis Edward Ross. - London:
Routledge and Kegan Paul, 1905. - 294 p. : (Wayfaring
Books)

47 BAKER, G. P.
        Mountaineering memories of the past / by G. P.
Baker. - 1951.

48 BAKEWELL, R.
        Travels ... in the Tarentaise and ... Grecian and
Pennine Alps and in Switzerland and Auvergne in 1820,
1821 and 1822/ by R. Bakewell. - London: Longmans,
1823. - 2v. : ill.

49 BALCH, Edwin Swift
        Mountain exploration/ by Edwin S. Balch. - Phila-
delphia: Geographical Club of Philadelphia, 1893. -
plates.
        (Bulletin of the Geographical Club of Philadelphia,
vol. 1, no. 1.)

50 _____ .
        Mount McKinley and mountain climber's proofs/ by
Edwin Swift Balch. - Philadelphia: Campion, 1914. -
142 p.
        See also COOK, Frederick Albert (220); BROWNE,
Delmore (131)

51 BALL, Benjamin Lincoln
        Three days on the White Mountains: being the peril-
ous adventure of Dr. B. L. Ball on Mount Washington
during October 25, 26 and 27, 1855/ written by himself. - Boston: N. Noyes, 1856. - 72 p.

52 BALL, John
        The Alpine guide/ ed. by John Ball. - London:
Longmans, 1863-68. - 4v.
        Reprinted in parts as Introduction to the Alpine guide
(London: Longmans, 1866); The central Alps (London:
Longmans, 1876); etc.

53 _____ .
        Introduction to "The Alpine club"/ John Ball. -
London: the Alpine Club, 1873.

54
_____.
　　Peaks, passes and glaciers/ ed. by John Ball. -
2nd ed. - London: 1862. - 2v. : ill., plates.
　　First pub. 1859.　"The summation of the 'golden
age' of mountaineering!　A classic still of sustained interest. " RHB.

55　BAND, George
　　Road to Ragoposhi/ by George Band. - London:
Hodder and Stoughton, 1955. - 192 p. : plates.
　　Story of the 1954 Cambridge University Mountaineer-
ing Club's expedition to the Karakorom in Northern Pak-
istan, its objective being Mt. Ragaposhi. Ed.

56　BANJA, K. C.
　　Darjeeling at a glance: descriptive and historical
Darjeeling and Sikkim, of Everest and Kongchonjunga ex-
peditions/ by K. C. Banja. - Darjeeling: Oxford Book
and Stationery, 1947. - 144 p. : ill.

57
_____.
　　Lure of the Himalaya:　embodying accounts of Mount
Everest expeditions by land and air/ by K. C. Banja. -
Darjeeling: Gilbert, 1944. - 255 p. : ill.

58
_____.
　　Mystic Tibet and the Himalaya/ by K. C. Banja. -
Darjeeling: Oxford Book & Stationery, 1948. - 306 p. :
ill.

59
_____.
　　Wonders of Darjeeling and the Sikkim Himalaya: ac-
counts all authentic/ by K. C. Banja. - Darjeeling:
Gilbert, 1945. - 198 p. : ill.

60　BANKS, Michael Edward Borg
　　Commando climber/ by Mike Banks. - London:
Dent, 1955. - 240 p. : plates.

61
_____.
　　Ragaposhi/ by Mike Banks. - Foreword by Field
Marshall Sir Gerald Templer. - London: Secker and
Warburg, 1959. - 238 p. : 24 plates, 3 maps.
　　A typical expedition account with anecdotes and the
physical problems of an ascent on a high mountain. Ed.

62
_____.
　　Snow commando/ by Mike Banks, illus. by Robin

Collomb. - London: Burke, 1961. - 192 p. : 8 plates, map. (Modern men of action series)

62a BARFORD, John Edward Quintus
Climbing in Britain/ by John Barford. - New York: Penguin, 1946. - 160 p. : plates. (Pelican Books)
"A Pelican book, sponsored by the British Mountaineering Council, to help the ever-increasing number of young climbers. Informative on technique, equipment, where to walk and climb, hostels and huts. " NBL.

63 BARKER, Ralph
The last Blue Mountain/ by Ralph Barker, with a foreword by John Hunt. - London: Chatto & Windus, 1959. - 212 p. : 22 plates, maps, tables.
Tragic story of the Oxford University Expedition to Haramosh in 1957. Ed.

BARNES, Malcolm, ed. <u>see</u> MOUNTAIN WORLD (659)

64 BARROW, John
Expeditions on the glaciers: including an ascent of Mount Blanc, Monte Rosa, Col du Geant and Mont Buet/ by a private of the Thirty-Eighth Artists', and member of the Alpine Club. - 1864. - 126 p.

65 _____ .
Mountain ascents in Westmoreland and Cumberland/ by John Barrow. - London: Sampson & Co., 1886. - 208 p.

66 BARRY, Martin
Ascent to the summit of Mont Blanc, Sept. 16 to 18, 1834/ by Martin Barry. - London: H. Teape & Son, 1835. - 40 p. : MS

BARTROPP, John <u>see</u> PILDITCH, Sir Philip Harold (755)

67 BASTERFIELD, George
Mountain lure/ by G. Basterfield. - 1947.

68 _____ .
Songs of the cragsman: words and music/ by G. Basterfield. - 1935.

69 BATES, Robert Hicks, ed.
Five miles high/ ed. by R. H. Bates. - London:

Hale, 1940. - 319 p. : ill. , plates.
   The story of an attack on the second highest moun-
tain in the world by the members of the First American
Karakoram Expedition, by R. H. Bates, C. S. Houston,
R. L. Burdsall and W. P. House. Ed.

70   .
   A study of the literature of the mountains and of
mountain climbing written in English/ by Robert Bates. -
Ann Arbor, Mich. : University Microfilms, 1947 (1951). -
Pub. no AC-1, 2093.
   A selective and comprehensive survey of the literary
and historical aspects of mountaineering literature. Pen-
etrating and informative, it constituted part of the author's
requirement for his Ph. D. Ed.

71 BAUER, Paul
   Himalayan campaign: the German attack on Kanchen-
junga; the second highest mountain in the world/ by Paul
Bauer, trans. from the German by Sumner Austin. -
London: Oxford University Press, 1937. - 174 p. : 92
ill. , maps.
   Describes two German attempts in 1929 and 1931.
Ed.

72   .
   Himalayan quest/ by P. Bauer; trans. by E. G.
Hall. - London: Nicolson and Watson, 1938. - 150 p. :
96 plates
   "This records the successful attacks of the German
parties on Sinioluchu and one of the Simvu peaks in Sikkim
in 1936, and the disaster which overwhelmed Dr. Wien's
party on Nanga Parbat in 1937. The photos are all notable, often magnificent. " Yakushi.

73   .
   Kanchenjunga challenge/ by Paul Bauer, foreword by
Sir John Hunt. - London: Kimber, 1955. - 202 p. : 11
plates.
   "Famous Bavarian expeditions to Kanchenjunga in
1929 and 1931, and the ascent of Sinidchu in 1936. " NBL.

74   .
   Siege of Nanga Parbat, 1856-1953/ by Paul Bauer;
trans. from the German by R. W. Rickmers with a preface by Sir John Hunt. - London: Hart-Davis, 1956. -
211 p. : plates.

Orig. pub. as Das Ringen um der Nanga Parbat (Munich: Suddt, 1955). "Complete survey of the attempts on Nanga Parbat including everything from the mid-nineteenth century explorations of Adolf Schlagintweit, the first European to see the peak, to H. Buhl's solo climb to the summit in 1953. " Yakushi.

75 BEACH, William N.
In the shadow of Mount McKinley/ by William N. Beach. - New York: The Derrydale Press, 1931. - 289 p. : ill. , map.

76 BECHERVAISE, John Mayston
Mountaineering/ by J. M. Bechervaise, illus. by Ronald Brooks. - Melbourne: University Press, 1971. - 32 p. : ill. (Life in Australia)
A very brief account of mountaineering on par with a popular magazine article by a new climber, meant only to arouse interest, mainly of junior readers. Ed.

77 BECHTOLD, Fritz
Nanga Parbat adventure: a Himalayan expedition/ by Fritz Bechtold, trans. by H. E. G. Tyndale. - London: Murray, 1935. - 93 p. : ill. , maps, 80 plates.
Orig. pub. as Deutsche um Nanga Parbat. "Account of the German 1934 expedition when 4 Europeans and 6 porters lost their lives. Adventure in text and photographs. " BRD.

78 BECKEY, Fred W.
Challenge of the North Cascades/ by Fred Beckey, maps by Dee Molenaar. - Seattle: the Mountaineers, 1969. - 280 p. : ill. , maps, ports.

79 BELL, James Horst Brunnerman
British hills and mountains/ ed. by J. H. B. Bell, in conjunction with E. F. Bozman and J. F. Blakeborough. - 3rd rev. ed. - London: Batsford, 1950. - 120 p. : 99 photos.
First pub. 1940. Though written by a mountaineer the aim and scope are too great for such a small book, resulting in being too general and intended for hill walkers rather than climbers. Ed.

80 _____ .
Progress in mountaineering: Scottish Hills to Alpine Peaks/ by J. H. B. Bell. - London: Oliver and Boyd,

1960. - 424 p. : plates, maps.
    "Three sections of climbs in the Alps and Britain; and two of technical instruction, by a Scottish climber with an extensive experience of his own hills in summer and winter. " NBL.

BENESCH, F. See CHRISTOMANOS, T. (178)

81 BENSON, Claude Ernest
    British mountaineering/ by C. E. Benson. - 2nd ed. - London: Routledge and Kegan Paul, 1914. - 224 p. First pub. 1909.

82 _____.
    Crag and hound in Lakeland/ by C. E. Benson. - London: Hurst and Blackett, 1902. - 313 p. : ill.

83 _____.
    Mountaineering ventures/ by C. E. Benson. - London: T. C. and E. C. Jack, 1928. - 224 p. : plates.

84 BENT, Allen Herbert
    A bibliography of the White Mountains/ by Allen H. Bent. - Boston: Appalachian Mountain Club, 1911. - 114 p. : ports.

85 _____.
    Early American mountaineers/ by Allen H. Bent. - Boston: 1913. Cover title, p. 45-67, plates.
    Reprinted from Appalachia, v. xiii. No. 1.

86 _____.
    Equipment for mountain climbing and camping/ by A. H. Bent, Ralph Lawson and Perceval Sayward. -

87 BENUZZI, Felice
    No picnic on Mt. Kenya/ by F. Benuzzi. - 2nd ed. - London: William Kimber, 1952. - 230 p. : plates, port.
    "Delightful account of a most spirited attempt on Mt. Kenya by escaped prisoners of war conveys the compelling attraction of mountains better than more orthodox books. " NBL.

87a BERE, Rennie
    The way to the mountains of the moon/ by Rennie Bere. - London: Arthur Barker, 1966. - 147 p. : maps, plates.

A description of the mountains of the moon in their African context by a mountain climber. The aspects of climbing form a background to an enjoyable book. Ed.

88 BERLEPSCH, Hermann Alexander von
     The Alps: or sketches of life and nature in the mountains/ by Hermann A. Von Berlepsch; a trans. by Leslie Stephens. - London: Longmans, 1861. - 407 p. : 17 plates from designs by Emil Rittmeyer.

89 BERNSTEIN, Jeremy
     Ascent: of the invention of mountain climbing and its practice/ by Jeremy Bernstein. - New York: Random House, 1965. - 124 p. : ill. , ports. , bibl.

89a BERTRAM, A.
     German tourism and mountaineering/ by A. Bertram. -

90 BHATTACHARJYA, Bidyapati
     Mountain sickness/ by B. Bhattacharjya. - Baltimore: Williams & Wilkins, 1964. - 58 p. : ill. , bibl.

91 BICKERDIKE, P.
     Rope climbing/ by P. Bickerdike. - Athletic publications, 1935. - 72 p.

92 BICKNELL, Peter
     British hills and mountains/ by Peter Bicknell. - London: Collins, 1947. - 47 p. : plates. (Britain in pictures, The British people in pictures)
     "British mountains viewed geologically, historically, aesthetically and athletically, by a climber who is also a connoisseur of the picturesque. " NBL.

     BLACKER, I., V. Stewart see FELLOWES, Peregrine
          Forbes Morant (313)

93 BLACKSHAW, Alan
     Mountaineering: from hill walking to alpine climbing/ by Alan Blackshaw. - 2nd ed. - Harmondsworth: Penguin Books, 1970. - 542 p. : 172 plates, ill. , maps.
     First pub. 1965. Without doubt the most modern and comprehensive book of equipment and instruction yet written. The photography and illustrations are exceptional. Ed.

BLAKEBOROUGH, J. F.   see   BELL, James H. B. (79)

94 BLAKENEY, Edward Henry, ed.
Peaks, passes and glaciers/ selected and annotated
by E. H. Blakeney. - London: Dent, 1926. - 365 p.
A selection, plus four additional papers from the
book of the same title by John Ball. Ed.

95 BLAKENEY, Thomas Sydney
Mountaineering and the British Royal family/ by
T. S. Blakeney. - London: The Alpine Club, 1953. -
10 p. : 3 plates. (Private circulation)

96 BLANCHET, F. R.
Mountaineering/ by F. R. Blanchet. - London: Lonsdale, 1934. - (Lonsdale library)

97 BOECK, Kurt
Himalaya-album/ by Kurt Boeck. - 1894.

98 BOELL, Jacques
High heaven/ by J. Boell; trans. from the French by
Dillys Owens. - London: Elek, 1947. - 126 p. : plates.
On mountaineering in the French Dauphine. Ed.

99 BONATTI, Walter
On the heights/ by Walter Bonatti; trans. from the
Italian by L. F. Edwards. - London: Hart Davis, 1964. -
248 p. : 16 plates.
Orig. pub. as Le mie montagne (Bolonga: Zauchelli,
1961).   A combination of rock climbing and mountaineering
from the classic problems of the Alps to the Himalayas
by probably the greatest Italian rock climber. Ed.

100 BONINGTON, Christian
Annapurna south face/ by Chris Bonington. - London:
Cassell, 1971. - 334 p. : ill. , 49 plates, ports.
Thrilling account of an expedition by a great moun-
taineer and photographer, combining personal narrative
with administrative details on how to outfit an expedition. Ed.

100a _____ .
Everest: south face/ by Chris Bonington. - London:
Hodder & Stoughton, 1973. - 352 p. : ill. , plates.
A detailed expedition with this book as its official
history.   The appendices include chapters on food, medicine, communication etc.   The photography is inspiring
and the text interesting. Ed.

101
_____.
    I chose to climb / by Chris Bonington, with a fore-word by Eric Shipton. - London: Gollancz, 1966. - 208 p. : front., 3 ill., map, 38 plates.
    The first part of the author's biography including his many attempts on the Eiger. An inspiring book, well illustrated and typical of the modern school combining technical climbing with expeditions. Ed.

102
_____.
    The next horizon: autobiography II / by Christian Bonington. - London: Gollancz, 1973. - 304 p. : 48 plates, ill., 13 maps.

BONNEY, Lorraine see BONNEY, Orin H. (103)

103 BONNEY, Orrin H.
    Field book: the Wind River Range, including Bridger, Glacier and Popo Ague wilderness areas, and the Wind River Reservation / by O. H. and Lorraine Bonney. - 2nd rcv. ed. - Houston: 1968. - 195 p. : 11 plates, ill., maps, ports.
    Includes the American rating system, climbing routes and back country. Ed.

104 BONNEY, Thomas George
    An ascent of the Grivda / by Thomas G. Bonney.

BORG, T. do see EGELER, Cornelius Geoffrey (286)

105 BORTHWICK, Alastair
    Always a little further / by Alastair Borthwick. - Glasgow: John Smith, 1969. - 221 p.

106 BOURRIT, Marc Theodore
    A Relation of the journey to the glaciers in the Duchy of Savoy / by M. T. Bourrit; trans. from the French by C. & F. Davy. - Norwich: 1775. - 264 p.

107 BOWIE, Ann
    Mick Bowie: the Hermitage years / by Ann Bowie. - Wellington, N. Z. : Reed, 1969. - 196 p. : ill., maps.

BOWIE, Mick see BOWIE, Ann (107)

108 BOZMAN, Ernest Franklin
    Mountain essays by famous climbers / ed. by E. F. Bozman. - London: Dent, 1928. - 254 p. : ill.
    See also BELL, James Horst Brunnerman (79)

109 BRAND, Charles
      Journal of a voyage to Peru: a passage across the
      Cordillera of the Andes in the winter of 1827, performed
      on foot in the snow; and a journey across the Pampas/
      by Lieut. Chas. Brand. - London: 1828. - plates.

      BRASHER, Christopher see HUNT, Sir Henry Cecil
          John (467)

110 BRENNER, F.
      Two years in Switzerland and Italy/ by F. Brenner.

111 BRIDGE, George, comp.
      Rock climbing in the British Isles, 1894-1970: a
      bibliography of guidebooks/ Reading: West Col Produc-
      tions, 1971. - 40 p.: ill., diagrs.
      A definitive work on Great Britain, which includes
      rare and privately published guides: in all 303 entries
      well presented. Ed.

112 BRIDGE, L. D.
      Mountain search and rescue in New Zealand/ by
      L. D. Bridge. - 2nd ed. - Wellington: Federated
      Mountaineering Clubs of New Zealand, 1962. - 225 p.:
      ill., maps, bibl.

113 _____.
          Safe climbing/ ed. by L. D. Bridge for the Taraua
      Tramping Club. - Wellington, N. Z.: Reed, 1947.

114 BRIDGES, George Wilson
      Alpine sketches/ by a member of the University of
      Oxford. - London: Longmans, 1814. - 312 p.

115 BRITISH MOUNTAINEERING COUNCIL
      Exposure/joint circular by the British Mountaineer-
      ing Council and Association of Scottish Climbing Clubs. -
      London: the Council, 1964. - 8 p.: (B. M. C. 380)

116 _____.
          Your rope. - London: the Council, 1965. - 4 p.

117 BRITISH STANDARDS INSTITUTION
      Specifications for mountaineering ropes--nylon: BS
      3104/ London: B. S. I., 1959.

117a _____.
          Specifications for climber's helmets: BS 4423/

London: B. S. I. , 1969.

118 BROCKEDON, William
Illustrations of passes of the Alps by which Italy
communicates with France, Switzerland and Germany/
by William Brockedon. - London: the Author, 1883. -
2 v.
"Plates of all the main passes, from the Maritime
Alps to the Brenner with first hand descriptions. " NBL

119 _____.
Journal of excursions in the Alps/ by William
Brockedon. - London: James Duncan, 1883. - 376 p.
Record of a foot traveler who did not aspire to
climbing! Covers passes in Savoy, Val d'Aosta, Dau-
phine, Grisons, the Oberland and Zermatt. Ed.

120 BROKE, G.
With sack and stock in Alaska/ by G. Broke.
1891. maps.

121 BRONGERSMA, Leo Daniel
To the mountains of the stars/ by L. D. Bron-
gersma and G. Venema; trans. from the Dutch by Alan
G. Readett. - London: Hodder and Stoughton, 1962. -
318 p. : 23 ill. , 48 plates, maps, bibl.
The Dutch expedition to the Antares mountains in
New Guinea. Ed.

122 BROUGHTON, Geoffrey, ed.
Climbing Everest: an anthology/ selected and ed.
by G. Broughton from the writings of the climbers them-
selves; illus. by W. H. Cooper and H. Somervell.
London: O. U. P. , 1960. - 149 p. : ill.

123 BROWER, David Ross, ed.
Manual of ski mountaineering/ ed. by David R.
Brower, for the National Ski Association of America. -
2nd ed. - Los Angeles: University of California Press,
1946. - 200 p. : ill. , plates.

124 BROWN, Joseph
The hard years: an autobiography/ by Joe Brown. -
London: Gollancz, 1967. - 256 p. : front. , 32 plates
(incl. port.)
A biography of a legend--the life of a "tiger" whose
climbs still rate among the hardest technical problems

in Britain. With accounts of expeditions to the Pamirs, Mustagh Tower and Kanchenjunga. Ed.

125   BROWN, Thomas Graham
      Brenva/ by T. G. Brown. - London: Dent, 1944. - 225 p. : 71 plates.
      "An account of a long term obsession with the Brenva face on the Italian side of Mt. Blanc; together with three splendid routes, planned and achieved between the wars. An elegance of design and splendid photographs. " NBL.

126   .
      Col Maudit and other climbs/ by Thomas Graham Brown. - London: 1933.

127   .
      Masherbrum, 1938/ by Thomas Graham Brown. - London: 1940.

128   .
      Mount Foraker/ by Thomas Graham Brown. - London: 1935.

129   .
      A new ascent of Piz Bernina/ by Thomas Graham Brown. - London: 1931.

130   .
      The first ascent of Mont Blanc/ by T. G. Brown and Sir Gavin Rylands De Beer. Pub. on the occasion of the centenary of the Alpine Club, with a foreword by Sir John Hunt. - London: Oxford University Press, 1957. - 460 p. : ill. , maps.

131   BROWNE, Belmore
      The conquest of Mount McKinley: the story of three expeditions through the Alaskan wilderness to Mount McKinley, America's highest and most inaccessible mountain/ by Belmore Browne, appendix by Herschel C. Parker. - New York and London: Putnam, 1913. - xvii, 381 p. : ill. , map.
      "Exposed Cook's falsification of the ascent of Mt. McKinley--one of the finest American books on mountaineering. " BRD.

132   BROWNE, G. F. (Bishop of Bristol)
      Off the mill: some occasional papers (on Alpine

subjects)/ by Bishop G. F. Browne. - 1895. - ill.

133 BROWNE, J. D. H.
Ten scenes in the last ascent of Mont Blanc: including five views from the summit/ sketched and lith-
ographed by the author. - London: Thos. McLean,
1853. - 13 p.

134 BRUCE, Charles Granville
The Assault of Everest, 1922/ by Brigadier Charles
Bruce. - London: Edward Arnold, 1924. - 337 p. :
plates, maps, ill.
"Sequel to Howard-Bury's Mount Everest--the reconnaissance; describes the climb when the 27,000 foot
mark was reached, and the first use of oxygen. Won-
derful prose by Leigh Mallory. " BRD.

135 .
Himalayan wanderer/ by Brigadier Charles Bruce. -
London: Maclehose, 1934. - 309 p. : 25 ill., port.
"This is the story of a great explorer's life: C. G.
Bruce. The big expeditions; Conway's exploration in the
Karakorum, Mummery's attack on Nanga Parbat, Long-
staff's success on Trisul, two Mount Everest expeditions,
etc. " Yakushi.

136 .
Kulu and Lahoul: an account of my latest climbing
journeys in the Himalaya/ by Brigadier Charles Bruce.
London: Edward Arnold, 1914. - 307 p. : ill., maps.
"Bruce has explored the Khargan, the Karakorum,
the Nankan ranges, Kumaon, Garhwal, and now also the
mountains of Kulu and Lahoul. " Yakushi.

137 .
Twenty years in the Himalayas/ by Brigadier Charles Bruce. - London: Arnold, 1910. - 035 p. : 60 ill.,
ports., maps.
"The author tells his quest experiences of explorations, climbing and travels in the Himalayan districts;
Sikkim, Nepal, Kumaon, Garhwal, Baltistan, Chitral,
etc. " Yakushi.

138 BRUNNING, Carl K.
Rock climbing and mountaineering/ by Carl K.
Brunning, with diagrams and maps drawn by R. G.
Twentyman. - 2nd ed. - London: Faber, 1946. - 87
p. : diagrs.

First pub. 1936.

139   BRYANT, Leslie Vickery
       New Zealanders and Everest/ by L. V. Bryant,
       with a foreword by Sir Edmund Hillary. - Wellington,
       Reed, 1953. - 48 p. : 2 ill.

140   BRYCE, James, Viscount Bryce
       Transcaucasia and Ararat/ by James Bryce. - 4th
       rev. ed. with a chapter on the recent history of the
       Armenian question. - London: Macmillan, 1896. -526 p.
       "Beautifully describes the mountain, lists legends
       regarding its inaccessibility and gives a detailed account
       of his successful expedition. " RHB.

141   BRYSON, H. C.
       Rock climbs around London/ by H. C. Bryson. -
       London: Brentford, 1936. - 28 p.

142   BUELER, William M.
       Mountains of the world; a handbook for climbers
       and hikers/ by William M. Bueler. - Wellington, N. Z.,
       Reed, 1969. - Englewood Cliffs, N. J., Prentice-Hall,
       1970. - 279 p. : 7 maps, ill.
       A comprehensive guide for a tourist or hiker limited
       to the beginner's level of rockclimbing, with useful ge-
       ographic information. Ed.

143   BUHL, Hermann
       Lonely challenge/ by Hermann Buhl; trans. from
       the German and with a foreword by Hugh Merrick. -
       New York: Dutton, 1956. - 318 p. : ill.

144   _____ .
       Nanga Parbat pilgrimage/ by Hermann Buhl; trans.
       from the German by Hugh Merrick. - London: Hodder
       and Stoughton, 1956. - 360 p. : 16 plates, 3 maps.
       Orig. pub. as Achtlausand drüber and drunter (Stut-
       tgart: Nymphenburger Verlagshandlung, 1954).

145   BULWEN, James Redford
       Extracts from my journal/ by James Redford Bul-
       wer. - Norwich: the Author, 1853. - 54 p. : 4 plates.
       "This little book was printed for private circulation
       only and there is a certain amount of confusion over
       the spelling of the surname. The bulk of the extract is
       devoted to an ascent of Mont Blanc. " Dawson's.

146 BURDSALL, Richard L.
        Men against the clouds: the conquest of Minya Kon-
ka/ by R. L. Burdsall and Arthur B. Emmons, with
contributions by Terris Moore and Jack Theodore Young,
etc. - New York: Harper, 1935. - 292 p. : maps,
plates.
        "The highest (24,900 foot) mountain climbed by A-
mericans in 1935. Has enthusiastic chapters on experiences on the climb and travelling to and from the
mountain. " BRD.

147 BURLINGHAM, Frederick
        How to become an alpinist/ by Fred Burlingham. -
Laurie, 1914. - 218 p. : ill.

148 BURMAN, Jose
        A peak to climb: the story of South African moun-
taineering/ by Jose Burman. - Cape Town: Struik,
1966. - 175 p. : maps.

        BURNABY, Mrs. Fred see Le BLOND, Elizabeth Alice
        Frances (527)

149 BURNET, Gilbert (Bishop of Salisbury)
        Burnet's travels: or ... letters to the Hon. Robert
Boyle, Esq.; containing an account of ... travelling
thro' Switzerland, Italy ... Germany, etc ... in 1685
and 1686/ by Gilbert Burnet. - New ed. - Ward and
Chandler, 1737. - 204 p.

149a BURNS, W. C.
        A short manual of mountaineering training/ by W.
C. Burns, F. Shuttleworth and J. E. B. Wright. - 6th
ed/ by P. F. Gentil. - London: Kaye and Ward, for
the Mountaineering Association, 1964.
        First pub. 1948.

150 BURPEE, Lawrence Johnstone
        Among the Canadian Alps: with four illustrations
in colour, 45 reproductions from photographs and 5
maps/ by L. J. Burpee. - London: John Lane,
1915.

151 BUSK, Douglas
        The delectable mountains/ by Douglas Busk. - the
sketches by Bridget Busk. - London: Hodder and Stough-

ton, 1946. - 274 p. : 47 plates.

152 _____.
      The fountain of the sun: unfinished journeys in Eth-
iopia and the Ruwenzori/ by Douglas Busk. - London:
Parrish, 1957. - 240 p. : plates, ill., maps, bibl.

153 BUZAK, Jakub
      Polish Himalayan expedition/ by Jakub Buzak. -
Glasgow: Mrs. J. Harasowsha, 1944. - ill.

154 BYLES, Marie Beuzeville
      By cargo boat and mountain: the unconventional ex-
periences of a woman on a tramp around the world/ by
M. B. Byles. - London: Seeley Service, 1931. - 315
p. : plates, ports.
      "An Australian authoress describes vividly her un-
conventional three year holiday spent climbing in Norway, the Canadian Rockies, the British Isles and New
Zealand. " BRD.

155 BYNE, Eric
      High Peak: the story of walking and climbing in
the Peak district/ by Eric Byne and Geoffrey Sutton. -
London: Secker and Warburg, 1966. - 256 p. : ill.

156 CAMERON, Una
      A good line/ written and illus. by Una Cameron. -
[S. L.]: privately printed, 1932. - 97 p. : ill.

157 CAMPBELL, J. I. , comp.
      A bibliography of mountains and mountaineering in
Africa/ comp. by J. I. Campbell. - Cape Town: School
of Librarianship, University of Cape Town, 1945. - 60
p. : front.
      406 references to books, articles and pamphlets on
mountaineering in South Africa and including a select
list of general books on mountaineering. Ed.

158 CAPE PENINSULA PUBLICITY ASSOCIATION
      Table mountain: some easy climbs to the summit/
Cape Peninsula Publicity Association. - Cape Town:
the Association, 1914. - 12 p.

159 CARR, Alfred
      Adventures with my Alpenstock and knapsack/ by
Alfred Carr. - York: 1875.

160   CARR, Herbert Reginald Culling, ed.
        The Mountains of Snowdonia in history, the sciences,
      literature and sport/ ed. by H. R. C. Carr and George
      A. Lister. - 2nd ed. - London: Crosby Lockwood,
      1948.
        "A many sided description.... Winthrop Young's
      picture of the friendly gatherings of climbers of all ages
      ... has a social as well as mountaineering interest. "
      NBL.

161   CASEWIT, Curtis W.
        The hiking-climbing handbook/ by Curtis W. Case-
      wit. - New York: Hawthorn Books, 1969. - 182 p.:
      ill. , ports.

162   _____.
        The Mountaineering handbook: an invitation to
      climbing/ by C. W. Casewit and Dick Pownall: Intro.
      by James Ramsay Ullman. - Philadelphia: Lippincott,
      1968. - 222 p.: 60 ill , bibl.

      CASSON, Cesar see HAYDEN, Sir Henry Hubert (417)

163   CATALOGUE OF EQUIPMENT FOR MOUNTAINEERS
        London: 1899.

164   CAVENDISH, Alfred Edward John
        Korea and the sacred White Mountain/ by A. E. J.
      Cavendish; with an account of the ascent of the White
      Mountain/ by Captain H. E. Goold-Adams. - London:
      Philips and Sons, 1894. - 224 p.: ill. , maps.

165   CENTRAL COUNCIL OF PHYSICAL RECREATION
        Safety on mountains/ by the staff of Plas y Brenin,
      the Snowdonia National Recreation Centre; illus. by
      Gordon F. Monsell. - London: Central Council of Phys-
      ical Recreation, 1961. - 41 p.: ill. , bibl.

166   CHANDLER, Edmond
        On the edge of the world (Persia)/ by Edmond Chand-
      ler. - 1919. - 278 p.: 35 ill. , map.

167   CHAPIN, Frederick H.
        Mountaineering in Colorado: the peaks about Estes
      Park/ by F. H. Chapin. - Boston: Appalachian Moun-
      tain Club, 1889. - 168 p.

168 CHAPMAN, Frederick Spencer
    Helvellyn to Himalayas/ by Frederick Chapman. -
London: Chatto & Windus, 1940. - 435 p. : ill.
    "Ascent of Chomolhari"; later published as Memoirs
of a mountaineer. GCPL. "Part autobiography--part
technical notes on mountaineering problems ... well
written. " BRD.

169   .
    Living dangerously: an account of the author's tra-
vels in the Arctic, the Himalayas and Malaya/ by Frederick Spencer Chapman. - London: Chatto & Windus,
1953. - 189 p. : plates, port.

170   .
    Memoirs of a mountaineer - Helvellyn to Hima-
laya. - Lhasa: the holy city/ by Frederick Spencer
Chapman. - London: the Reprint Society, 1945. -
446 p. : ill. , maps, plates.
    Rev. ed. pub. London: Chatto and Windus, 1951.

171 CHARLES, Wyndham
    A mountain and a man: Sherpa Tenzing/ by W.
Charles. - Rev. ed. - London: Blackie, 1969. - 14 p. :
ill. (Junior biographies)

172 CHASE, Charles H.
    Alpine climbers/ by Charles H. Chase.
London: 1888.

173 CHEEVER, George Barrell
    Wanderings of a pilgrim in the shadow of Mont
Blanc and the Jungfrau Alp/ by George Cheever. - London and Glasgow: William Collins, 1847. - 367 p.
    Also pub. as The pilgrim in the shadow of the Jung-
frau, 1846.

CHEVALLEY, Gabriel see DITTERT, Rene (260)

CHEVERST, W. see SCOTT, D. K. (848)

174 CHORLEY, Katherine Campbell, Baroness Chorley
    Hills and highways/ by Katherine Chorley. - Lon-
don: Dent, 1928. - 232 p. : ill.

175   .
    Lakeland: a playground for Britain/ ed. by K.
Chorley. - London: Barnow, 1930. - 30 p. : ill. , map.

176 .
      Manchester made them: reminiscences/ K. Chorley. - London: Faber and Faber, 1950. - 288 p.

177 CHOUINARD EQUIPMENT
      Catalogue/ by Yvon Chouinard and Tom Frost; photographs by Tom Frost and others. - Santa Barbara, California: Sand Dollar Press, 1970's. - 72 p.: 18 plates, ill.
      A guide to equipment for rock climbing and an explanation of its use. A most enthusiastic use of photos; a rock climbing manual in itself. Ed.

178 CHRISTOMANNOS, T.
      The Dolomites/ by T. Christomannos and F. Benesch. - 3rd ed. - Vienna: 191?. - ill., maps.

CHURCHILL, G. C. see GILBERT, J. (362)

CLARK, Charles see CLARK, Jane Inglis (179)

179 CLARK, Jane Inglis
      Pictures and memories: reminiscences of William Inglis Clark and his son Charles Clark/ J. I. Clark. - Edinburgh: Moray Press, 1938. - 91 p.

180 CLARK, Leonard Francis
      Marching wind/ by L. F. Clark. - London: Hutchinson, 1955. - 347 p.: plates.
      An account of the author's experiences in Northern Tibet. Ed. "In 1949 the author set out to find Amne Machin--a fabled mountain reputedly higher than Everest. A good yarn of how he found and measured it, but factually inaccurate." BRD.

181 CLARK, Ronald William
      The Alps/ by R. W. Clark. - New York: Knopf, 1973.

182 .
      Come climbing with me/ by Ronald Clark; illus. by T. K. Beck. - London: Muller, 1955. - 160 p.: (Junior Sportman's Library)

183 .
      The day the rope broke/ by R. W. Clark. - London: Secker and Warburg, 1965. - 221 p.: 4 plates.
      The story of the first ascent of the Matterhorn by

Edward Whymper and his tragic party in 1865. Gathered from contemporary sources and original documents. Ed.

184 _____.
The early alpine guides/ by R. W. Clark. - London: Phoenix, 1949. - 208 p. : ports.
"A series of short biographies based on the pioneers of the Alps, mountaineers' narratives and alpine journals. Well illustrated with reproductions of original illustrations. " BRD.

185 _____.
An eccentric in the Alps: the story of the Rev. W. A. B. Coolidge, the great Victorian mountaineer/ by R. W. Clark. - London: Museum Press, 1959. - 224 p. : ill. , 16 plates.

186 _____.
Great moments in mountaineering/ by R. W. Clark. - illus. by Thomas K. Beck. - London: Phoenix House, 1956. - 126 p. : ill.
For children

187 _____.
Great moments in rescue/ by R. W. Clark. - with 10 drawings by Dick Hart. - London: Phoenix House, 1959. - 128 p. : ill.
For children

188 _____.
Mountaineering in Britain: a history from the earliest times to the present day/ by R. W. Clark and Edward Charles Pyatt. - London: Phoenix House, 1957. - 288 p. : 104 plates, bibl.

189 _____.
Picture history of mountaineering/ by R. W. Clark. - Hulton, 1956. - 142 p. : 352 ill. (Picture Histories, ed. by Edward Halton)
Overwhelming number of photographs covering mountaineering up to and including Mt. Everest. Best of the general histories of the period to 1900. Ed.

190 _____.
Six great mountaineers/ by R. W. Clark. - London: Hamilton, 1956. - 203 p. : 6 plates, bibl.

Contents: Edward Whymper, A. F. Mummery, J. Norman Collie, George Leigh Mallory, Geoffrey Winthrop Young, Sir John Hunt. Ed.

191 _____ .
The Splendid hills: the life and photographs of Vittorio Sella, 1859-1943/ by R. W. Clark. - with reproductions and ports. London: Phoenix House, 1948. - 118 p.
"Sella was one of the greatest Italian Alpine photographers. The greater part of this book is occupied by large reproductions of his works in the Alps, Alaska, Africa, Himalaya and Karakorum. " Yakushi.

192 _____ .
The true book about mountains/ illus. by F. Stokes May. - London: Muller, 1957. - 143 p. : ill.
For children

193 _____ .
The Victorian mountaineers/ by R. W. Clark. - London: Batsford, 1953. - 23 p. : 45 plates.
" ... much interesting information not available elsewhere. " NBL.

194 CLARK, Simon
The puma's claw/ by Simon Clark. - London: Hutchinson, 1959. - 223 p. : 3 maps, 17 plates.
Report of the Cambridge Andean Expedition in 1957 to the Cuzco Department, Pumasillo, Peru. Interesting. Ed.

CLARK, William Inglis see CLARK, Jane Inglis (179)

195 CLEARNE, John
Sea cliff climbing in Britain/ by J. Cleare and Robin Collomb. - London: Constable, 1973. - 189 p. : ill. , maps, plates.

196 CLEMENTI, (Mrs.) Cecil
Through British Guiana to the summit of Roraima/ by Mrs. Cecil Clementi. - New York: 1920?. - 236 p. : 14 ill. , map.

197 [No entry]

198 CLISSOLD, Frederick
Narrative of an ascent to the summit of Mont Blanc: with an appendix upon the sensations experienced at great

elevations/ by Frederick Clissold. - London: Riving-
tons & Cochran, 1823. - 56 p.
"The first of many books by Englishmen describing
their ascent of Mt. Blanc--when climbers wore veils
and carried six foot batons and six guides per person
were de rigueur. " NBL.

199　COCKBURN, Henry
Catalogue of books in the library of the Alpine
Club/ by Henry Cockburn. - with lists of accessions/
compiled by A. J. MacKintosh. - Edinburgh: University
Press, 1899.
First pub. London: 1880. A multi-language direct-
ory of books published prior to 1880 in author and
subject order. Useful from the historical viewpoint. Ed.

200　COLEMAN, Arthur Philemon
The Canadian Rockies: new and old trails/ by A.
P. Coleman. - London: Fisher Unwin, 1911. - 383 p.:
ill.
"Great freshness and charm, telling of a lifetime
of pleasant climbing in the Canadian Rockies. " RHB.

201　COLEMAN, J. C.
The mountains of Killarney/ J. C. Coleman. -
Dundalk: Dundalga Press, 1948. - 60 p.: plates.

202　COLLET, Leon William
The structure of the Alps/ by Leon Collet. - 2nd
ed. - London: Edward Arnold, 1935. - 289 p.: 12
plates.
First pub. 1927.

203　COLLIE, John Norman
Climbing on the Himalaya and other mountain
ranges/ by John N. Collie. - Edinburgh: David Doug-
las, 1902. - 315 p.: plates.
"A great climber, friend of Slingsby, Hastings and
Mummery, who lost his life on this expedition and to
whom this book is dedicated. " RHB.
See also STUTFIELD, Hugh E. M. (933)

204　COLLINS, Francis Arnold
Mountain climbing/ by F. A. Collins. - New York
& London: Century Co., 1924. - 314 p.: ill., plates,
bibl.
"From the historical viewpoint of early climbers

to developments in 1924, including equipment and training, to an account of mountain conquest throughout the
world. It includes a chapter on mountain tragedies. "
BRD.

205 COLLOMB, Robin Gabriel
Alpine points of view, or, contemporary scenes
from the Alps, including some observations and opinions
of an itinerant Alpinist/ by R. G. Collomb. - London:
Spearman, 1961. - 231 p.: ill., maps.

206 _____.
Chamonix--Mont Blanc/ by R. G. Collomb. - London: Constable, 1969.

207 _____.
A dictionary of mountaineering/ by R. G. Collomb. -
London: Blackie and Son, Ltd., 1957. - 175 p. 100
drawings, bibl.
"Definitions, names and terms and their explana-
tions, used by English speaking mountaineers particularly in Britain and the Continent. " Subtitle.

208 _____.
Mountains of the Alps: tables of summits over
3,500 metres with geographical and historical notes and
tables of selected lesser heights/ compiled by R. G.
Collomb and Peter Crew. - Reading: West Col Productions, 1971. - 2 vols.
Contents: Vol. 1 Western Alps, Mediterranean to
the Simplonpars and Grimselpass. Vol. 2 Central and
Eastern Alps.

209 _____.
Zermatt and district, including Saas Fee/ by R. G.
Collomb. - London, Constable, 1969.
See also BANKS, Michael Edward Borg (62);
CLEARE, John (195)

210 CONWAY, S.
Preparation for the mountain/ by S. Conway. - Canterbury Mountaineering Club of New Zealand, 1953.

211 CONWAY, William Martin (Baron Conway of Allington)
Aconcagua and Tierradel Fuego: a book of climbing, travel and exploration/ by William Conway. - London: Cassell, 1902. - 252 p.: 27 ill., map.

212
        .
        The Alps / by W. M. Conway: painted by A. D.
McCormick. - London: Black, 1904. - 294 p.
        Also pub. with 23 ill. , from photographs by L.
Edna Walter. - London: Black, 1910.

213
        .
        The Alps from end to end / by W. M. Conway, with
100 full page illus. by A. D. McCormick. - Westminster: Constable, 1895. - 403 p. : ill.
        "The record of a 3 month expedition from the Mari-
time Alps to the Gross Glockner, traversing peaks and
passes ... with 2 Alpine guides and 2 Gurkhas whom
he wished to train for Himalayan work. " NBL.

214
        .
        Autobiography of a mountain climber / by W. M.
Conway. - London: Jonathan Cape, 1936. - (Travellers
series)
        Previously published in 1920 under title Mountain
memories. Ed.

215
        .
        The Bolivian Andes: a record of climbing and ex-
ploration in the Cordillera Real in the years 1898 and
1900 / by William Martin Conway. - New York: Harper,
1901. - 405 p. : ill.

216
        .
        Climbing and exploration in the Karakoram - Hima-
layas / by William Martin Conway, with three hundred
illustrations by A. D. McCormick. - London: Fisher
Unwin, 1894. - 3 vols. : maps.
        "One of the greatest journeys of mountain explora-
tion, Conway climbed a peak of 23,000 feet and traversed 3 of the longest known glaciers outside the polar
regions. " NBL.

217
        .
        Episodes in a varied life: reminiscences / by W.
M. Conway. - London: Country Life, 1932. - viii, 276
p. : plates, port.

218
        .
        The first crossing of Spitzbergen: being an account
of an inland journey of exploartion / by W. M. Conway. -
London: Dent, 1897. - 371 p. : plates, maps.

With contributions by J. W. Gregory, A. Trevor-Battye and E. J. Garwood.

219 _____.

Mountain memories: a pilgrimage of romance / by W. M. Conway. - London: Cassell, 1920. - 282 p. : 16 plates.

"A biography from the Breithorn to Tierra del Fuego which includes his expeditions to Kashmir, Spitzbergen and South America. Written on impulse of an intense personal and emotional nature. " BRD.

220 COOK, Frederick Albert

To the top of the continent: discovery, exploration and adventure in sub-arctic Alaska: the first ascent of Mt. McKinley, 1903-1906 / by Frederick Albert Cook. - New York: Doubleday, 1908. - 321 p. : ill., maps.

Cook's claims that this was the first ascent of Mt. McKinley was later proved to be false--by Belmore Browne. (131) Ed.

221 COOLIDGE, William Augustus Brevoort

The alpine career, 1868-1914 of Frederick Gardiner / by W. A. B. Coolidge, 1920.

222 _____.

Alpine studies / by W. A. B. Coolidge. - London: Longmans, 1912. - 307 p. : 16 ill.

223 _____.

The Alps in nature and history / by W. A. B. Coolidge. - London: Methuen, 1908. - 440 p. : ill., maps.

"In scholarly and critical fashion deals with topographical divisions ... and modern ascents. Nowhere in English is there such an authoritative and complete study of this huge subject. " RHB. Contains an early history of mountain ascents prior to 1850. Ed.

224 _____.

Climb in the Alps, made in ... 1865 to 1900 / by W. A. B. Coolidge. - London: n. d.

225 _____.

Swiss travels and Swiss guidebook / by W. A. B. Coolidge.

"Lacks the broad interest and elasticity of style of The Alps.... " RHB.

226 CORBETT, Edmund V.
    Great true mountaineering stories / selected and in-
troduced by E. V. Corbett. - London: Arco, 1957. -
227 p. : (Junior Book)

227 COVERLEY-PRICE, Victor
    An artist among mountains / with 33 illustrations
from drawings by the author. - London: Hale, 1957.
231 p. : 32 plates.

228 COXHEAD, Eileen Elizabeth
    One green bottle / by E. E. Coxhead. - London:
Faber, 1955. - 281 p.

229 CRABB, Edmund William
    The challenge of the summit: stories of mountains
and men / by Edmund William Crabb. - London: Paternoster Press, 1957. - 152 p. : 16 plates.

230 CRAWFORD, Robert
    Across the Pampas and Andes / by Robert Crawford,
with illustrations by F. W. and E. Whymper. - London:
1884. - 344 p. : ill.

    CREASEY, C. H. see EVE, Arthur Stewart (300)

231 CREW, Peter
    Encyclopaedic dictionary of mountaineering / by
Peter Crew. - London: Constable, 1968. - 140 p. : ill.,
maps, 16 plates, bibl.
    An extended glossary of terms which has some worth
as a training manual, but is of more use for the non-
climber who wishes to understand the literature. Ed.
    See also COLLOMB, Robin Gabriel (208); SOPER,
Jack (909)

    CROOK, W. M. see JONES, Owen Glynne (492)

232 CROSS, Roselle Theodore
    My mountains / by Roselle Theodore Cross. - n. p. :
Stratford, 1921.
    "In the Rocky Mountains, the author writes of his
appreciation of living with mountains as neighbours, of
camping in and climbing them. " BRD.

233 CUMMING, C. F. Gordon
    From the Hebrides to the Himalayas: a sketch of

eighteen months' wanderings in western isles and eastern
highlands/ by C. F. Gordon Cumming. - London:
1876. - 2 vols.

234 _____ .
Granite crags/ by C. F. Gordon Cumming. - Edin-
burgh and London: 1884. - 384 p. : 8 ill., map.
"Yosemite and Sierra Nevada." Dawson's.

235 CUNNINGHAM, Carus Dunlop
The pioneers of the Alps/ by C. D. Cunningham
and W. de W. Abney. - London: Sampson, 1885. -
287 p. : ports., limited ed. of 50 copies.
"Brief descriptions of the outstanding guides from
Balmat to Burgener; illustrated with remarkable photographs. " NBL.

236 DANIEL, Giotto
Buddhists and glaciers of Western Tibet/ by Giotto
Daniell/ - London, 1935.

237 DARVILL, D. F. T.
Mountaineering medicine/ by D. F. T. Darvill.

238 DAUNT, Archilles
Crag, glacier and avalanche: narratives of daring
and disaster/ by Archilles Daunt. - London: Nelson,
1889. - 212 p. : 13 ill.

239 DAVENPORT, Eugene
Vacation on the trail: personal experiences in the
higher mountain trails with complete directions for the
outfitting of inexpensive expeditions/ by Eugene Davenport. - London: Macmillan, 1923. - 101 p. : ill. (Open
country books)
"Describes the essentials of camping in the higher
mountain trails of the Rocky Mountains. " BRD.

240 DAVIDSON, Art
The coldest climb: the winter ascent of Mt. Mc-
Kinley/ by Art Davidson. - London: Bodley Head,
1969. - 218 p. : ill., 16 plates
Also pub. New York: Curtis, 1972, under title:
Minus one hundred forty-eight degrees. The 1967 ex-
pedition to Mt. McKinley where one man died on the
first day. The book records every emotion, panic,
quarrel and hysterical moment of a harrowing expedition.
Ed.

241 _____.
Minus one hundred forty-eight degrees: the winter
assault of Mt. McKinley/ by Art Davidson. - New York:
Curtis, 1972.
Also pub. under title: The coldest climb (see 240).

DAVIDSON, Mavis see HEWITT, Rodney (431)

242 DAVIES, Joseph Sanger
Dolomite strongholds: the last untrodden Alpine
peaks/ by Joseph Sanger Davies. - Bell, 1896. - 176
p. : ill. , map.
"Accounts of ascents of the Croda di Lago, the Little and Great Zinnen, the Cinque Torri, the Fünffinger-
spitze, the Langkofel. " Subtitle.

243 DAVIS, John
Rope and rucksack/ ed. by John Davis. - Sydney:
Angus & Robertson, 1969. - 128 p.: Plates, ill. , maps.
Comprehensive work on all aspects of outdoor life
with detailed sections on rock climbing, canyoning, ski
touring, canoeing. Especially good in photography and
illustration. Ed.

244 DEACOCK, Antonia
No purdah in Padam: the story of the Women's
overland Himalayan expedition, 1958/ by Antonia Deacock. - London: Harrap, 1960. - 208 p.: 11 plates,
2 maps.
More of a travel book, but does include non-serious
climbing. A success for women's liberation. Ed.

245 DeBEER, Sir Gavin Rylands
Alps and elephants: Hannibal's march/ by Sir Gavin DeBeer. - New York: 1956. - 123 p.: 14 ill.
"There is a map of the route by which Hannibal
crossed the Alps and became thereby a very early alpinist. " Dawson's.

246 _____.
Alps and men: pages from forgotten diaries of
travellers and tourists in Switzerland/ by Sir Gavin De-
Beer. - London: Edward Arnold, 1932. - 256 p.: 16
plates.

247 _____.
Early travellers of the Alps/ by Gavin DeBeer. -

London: Sidgwock & Jackson, 1930. - 204 p. : ill. ,
maps, plates.

248 _____ .
Travellers in Switzerland: 1941-45, a chronological
list of authors who have travelled in Switzerland with
bibliographical references to their works/ - by Sir Gavin DeBeer. - London: Oxford University Press, 1949. -
583 p.
See also BROWN, Thomas Graham (130)

249 DENMAN, Earl
Alone to Everest/ by Earl Denman. - London: Collins, 1954. - 190 p. : ill. , 4 plates. (Fontana Book No.
126)
"A young naive Canadian, after rehearsal on eight
peaks in the Belgian Congo, sneaks into Nepal and tries
to carry out his ambition. His inevitable failure dis-
credits his criticism of large expeditions, the use of
oxygen and the injection of nationalism into mountaineering. " BRD.

250 DENT, Clinton Thomas
Above the snow line: mountaineering sketches between 1870 and 1880 (a biography)/ by C. T. Dent. -
London: Longmand, 1884. - 327 p. : 2 engravings, ill.
"Not as well written as some of Freshfield's work,
but still has interest and gives a realistic account of
climbing in the '70's and '80's. " RHB.

251 _____ .
Equipment for mountaineers: report of a special
committee on equipment for mountaineers/ by C. T.
Dent, W. M. Conway and J. H. Wicks. - London: Spottiswoode, 1892. - 36 p.

252 _____ .
Influence of science on mountaineering: (a paper
read before the Royal Institution of Great Britain)/ by
Clinton T. Dent. - n. p. : privately printed, 1895. - 9 p.

253 _____ .
Mountaineering/ by C. T. Dent; with contributions
by W. M. Conway and others. - London: Longmans,
1892. - 481 p. : ill. (Badminton Library)

254 DESIO, Ardito
Ascent of K2, second highest peak in the world/ by

Ardito Desio, trans. from the Italian by David Moore. -
London: Elek Books, 1955. - 239 p. : 24 plates, map.
Orig. pub. as La Conquista del K2 (Milan: Gar-
zanti, 1955); also pub. as Victory over K2. "Complete
and authoritative book for the expert; being too forma-
lised and detailed for the armchair mountaineer, except
for chapter on the summit. Should be compared with
Houston's book. " BRD.

255 DIAS, John
The Everest adventure: story of the second Indian
expedition/ by John Dias. - Delhi: Publications Divi-
sion, Ministry of Information and Broadcasting, 1965. -
63 p. : ill.

256 DIEMBERGER, Kurt
Summits and secrets/ by Kurt Diemberger; trans.
from the German by Hugh Merrick. - London: Allen &
Unwin, 1971. - 344 p. : 54 plates, ill., maps.
Rightly claimed as the finest piece of mountaineer-
ing literature written; includes the Eiger, Matterhorn,
Tirich West, and Broad Peak, as well as an account of
Hermann Buhl. Ed.

257 DINGLE, Graeme
Two against the Alps/ by G. Dingle. - Christchurch,
N. Z. : Whitcombe & Tombs, 1972. - 153 p. : map, 9
plates.
The first winter traverse of the southern Alps of
New Zealand by the author and Jill Tremain. Involves
walking and climbing by one of New Zealand's great
climbers. Ed.

258 DISLEY, John
Tackle mountaineering this way/ by J. Disley with
line drawings by Bordon Mansell. - 2nd ed. London:
Paul, 1968. - 127 p. : ill.

259 _____.
Tackle climbing this way/ by J. Disley. - London:
Stanley Paul, 1959. - 127 p. : ill., plates, maps, bibl.

260 DITTERT, Rene
Forerunners to Everest: the story of the two Swiss
expeditions of 1952/ by R. Dittert, Gabriel Chevalley
and Raymond Lambert; trans. from the French by Malcolm Barnes. - London: Allen & Unwin, 1954. - 236 p. :

8 plates, 2 maps.

"... when the West CWM was penetrated for the
first time ... the South Col reached and Lambert and
Tenzing got to within 1,000 feet of the summit. " NBL.

261   DIXON, Christopher Michael
     Rockclimbing/ by C. M. Dixon; with a foreword by
the President of the British Mountaineering Council,
London. - 2nd ed. - London: Educational productions,
1968. - 48 p. : ill. , bibl. (Know the game series)
     Basic knowledge that every climber must know,
otherwise out of date. Ed.

262   DOCHARTY, William McKnight
     A selection of some 900 British and Irish mountain
tops/ by W. M. Docharty. - n. p. : privately printed,
1954. - 124 p. : ill.
     Supplement. - n. p. : privately printed, 1962. - 2
vols. - ill.
     Also pub. Edinburgh: Darien Press, 1953.

DOCK, W. see GESNER, Conrad (361)

DODDERIDGE, M. see WHYMPER, Edward (1078)

DOIG, Desmond see HILLARY, Sir Edmund Percival
    (435)

263   DOUGHTY, J. H.
     Hill-writings/ collected by H. M. Kelly, ed. by
J. H. Doughty. - Manchester: Rucksack Club, 1937. -
150 p.
     See also KELLY, H. M. (495)

264   DOUGLAS, John Scott
     Summits of adventure: the story of famous moun-
tain climbs and mountain climbers/ by John Scott Douglas. - London: Muller, 1955. - 227 p. : 16 plates,
bibl.
     "A history of mountaineering from Mont Blanc to
Everest intended for teenagers; some of the accounts are
vivid and thrilling. " BRD.

265   DOUGLAS, John Sholto (8th Marquis of Queensbury)
     The spirit of the Matterhorn/ by John S. Douglas. -
London: W. Mitchell, 1881. - 31 p.
     "Verse. " British Museum.

266 DOUGLAS, William Orville
Beyond the high Himalayas: an account of a journey
to Afghanistan and Ladakh/ by William O. Douglas. -
London: Gollancz, 1953. - 352 p.

267 _____.
Exploring the Himalayas/ by William O. Douglas. -
New York: Random House, 1958. - 177 p. : ill. (World
landmarks books)

268 _____.
Of men and mountains/ by William O. Douglas. -
London: Gollancz, 1951. - 338 p.
"Climbs in the Rockies by a justice of the U.S.
Supreme Court. " NBL.

269 DOWNER, Arthur Cleveland
Mountaineering ballads/ by A. C. Downer. - London: Charles Murray, 1905. - 47 p.

270 DRASDO, Harold
Eastern crags/ by Harold Drasdo. - Ambleside:
Fell and Rock Climbing Club of the English Lake Dis-
trict, 1959. - 193 p. : ill. , tables.

271 DUDLEY, Ernest
Rangi: highland rescue dog/ by Ernest Dudley. -
London: Harvill Press, 1970. - 126 p. : plates.
Written in narrative form, closely resembling a
novel with first-hand experience. Aimed at a teenage
audience. Ed.

272 DuFAUR, Freda
Conquest of Mt. Cook and other climbs: an account
of four seasons mountaineering on the Southern Alps of
New Zealand/ by Freda DuFaur. - London: Allen and
Unwin, 1915. - 250 p. : plates.

273 DUFFERIN, Lord
Letters from high altitudes/ by Lord Dufferin.

274 DUNN, Robert
The shameless diary of an explorer/ by Robert
Dunn. - New York: 1907. - 297 p. : ill. , map.
"An attempt on Mt. McKinley. " Dawson's.   "Pun-
gent, colourful, jerky prose; however, a good example
of early American mountaineering literature. " RHB.

275 DUNSHEATH, Joyce
Afgan quest: the story of their Abingor Afghanistan
expedition in 1960/ by J. Dunsheath and Eleanor Baillie. - London: Harrap, 1961. - 239 p. : ill. , map.
"Account of the Women's expedition to the western-
most Hindu-Kush. " Yakushi.

276 _____.
Guest of the Soviets: Moscow and the Caucasus,
1957/ by Joyce Dunsheath. - 183 p. : 6 plates, map,
bibl.

277 _____.
Mountains and memsahibs/ by the members of the
Alsinger Himalayan Expedition, 1956; foreword by Mrs.
Pandit. - London: Constable, 1956. - 198 p. : 8 plates.

278 DUNSTAN, Ruth M.
Mountaineers/ by Ruth M. Dunstan. - London: Society for the Propagation of the Gospel in Foreign Parts,
1961. - 38 p.
Lesson material for children, incorporating 5 stories
of mountaineers. Ed.

279 DURHAM, William Edward
Summer holidays in the Alps, 1895-1914/ by W. E.
Durham. - London: Fisher Unwin, 1915. - 207 p. : ill.

280 DURRIR, C.
Mt. Blanc/ by C. Durrir. - Paris: 1897.
Probably written in French; bibliographical details
lacking. Ed.

281 DUTTON, E. A. T.
Kenya mountains/ by E. A. T. Dutton; with an introduction by Hillaire Belloc. - London: Cape, 1929. -
ill. , maps.

282 DYRENFURTH, Norman
To the third pole: the history of the high Himalaya/
by Norman Dyrenfurth; trans. from the German by Hugh
Merrick. - London: Laurie, 1955. - 233 p. : plates, 49
ill. , bibl.
Orig. pub. as Zum dritter Pol. The definitive work
on the Himalayan region from the mountaineering viewpoint. Gives a history till 1953 with scientific and geological details. Ed.

283 EBERLI, Henry
        An English mountaineer: A. W. Moore / by Henry
        Eberli. - Whitby, 1919.

284 ECKENSTEIN, Oscar
        The Karakorams and Kashmir / by Oscar Ecken-
        stein. - London: Fisher Unwin, 1896. - 254 p. : ill.
        "Personal experiences as a member of Conway's
        Karakoram expedition in 1892. " Yakushi.

284a EDELRID WORKS
        A guide to mountaineering ropes. - Isny, West Ger-
        many: Edelrid Works, 1960's. - 66 p.

285 EDWARDS, Amelia Blandford
        Untrodden peaks and unfrequented valleys: a mid-
        summer ramble in the Dolomites / by A. B. Edwards. -
        2nd ed. - London: Routledge and Kegan Paul, 1890. -
        339 p. : ill. , plates.
        First pub. 1873.

    EDWARDS, Menlove see SUTTON, Geoffrey (955)

286 EGELER, Cornelius Geoffrey
        The untrodden Andes: climbing adventures on the
        Cordillera Blanca, Peru / by C. B. Egeler in co-
        operation with T. de Borg; trans. by W. E. James. -
        London: Faber and Faber, 1955. - 203 p. : plates,
        ports.

287 EGGLER, Albert
        The Everest-Lhotse adventure / by Albert Eggler;
        trans. from the German by Hugh Merrick. - London:
        Allen and Unwin, 1957. - 223 p. : 24 plates, ill. , maps.
        Orig. pub. as Gipfel über den Wolken. "Account of
        the first ascent of Lhotse and of the second and third
        ascent of Mount Everest in 1956 by the Swiss expedition
        led by the author. " Yakushi.

288 EISELIN, Max
        The ascent of Dhaulagiri / by Max Eiselin; trans.
        from the German by E. N. Dowman. - London: Oxford
        University Press, 1961. - 159 p. : plates.
        "Account of the Swiss Dhaulagiri expedition of 1960.
        The author, leader of the expedition, was also the lea-
        der of the 1958 expedition. " Yakushi.

289   ELMS, Frances Raymond
      Mountains of the world: stories and pictures of the
great mountain ranges of the world/ by F. R. Elms. -
Manchester: Whitman, 1942. - 80 p. : maps.
      "Description and history of twelve mountain ranges
and two peaks for juvenile readers. " BRD.

      EMMONS, Arthur B.   see   BURDSALL, Richard L.
         (0146)

290   ENGEL, Claire Elaine
      History of mountaineering in the Alps/ by Claire
E. Engel. - London: Allen and Unwin, 1950. - 296 p. :
plates.
      "Though marred by inaccuracies, this survey con-
tains a good deal of historical material not available
elsewhere. " NBL.

291   .
      Mont Blanc/ ed. by C. E. Engel. - London: Allen
& Unwin, 1965.
      "An anthology of prose and poetry. " GCPL.   Favors
the literary aspects of mountains, but includes many extracts from mountaineers and climbers. Ed.

292   .
      Mountaineering in the Alps: a historical survey/
by Claire E. Engel. - New ed. ; totally rev. and enl.
with a foreword by Lord Hunt. - London: Allen and
Unwin, 1971. - 318 p. : plates, ill.

293   .
      They came to the hills/ by Claire E. Engel. - Lon-
don: Allen and Unwin, 1952. - 275 p. : plates. (Studies
of British mountaineers)

294   ENGLEHARD, Georgia
      Peterli and the mountain/ by Georgia Engelhard. -
Philadelphia: 1954. - 40 p. : ill.
      "Based on a true story of a cat who really climbed
the Matterhorn--or so it says. " Dawson's.

295   ESCARRA, Jean
      Himalayan assault: the French Himalayan expedi-
tion, 1936/ by J. Escarra and others; trans. from the
French by Nea A. Morin. - London: Methuen, 1938. -
203 p. : 48 plates, 3 maps.

"An account of the first French Himalayan expedition to
the Hidden Peak (Gasherbrum I) of 1936. They failed
owing to circumstances beyond human control. " Yakushi.

EVANS, Arthur see EVANS, Joan (300)

296 EVANS, Charles
Eye on Everest: a sketchbook of the great Everest
expedition/ by C. Evans. - London: Dobson, 1955. -
123 p. : ill.
"This sketchbook gives the author's personal impres-
sion of the 1953 Mount Everest expedition. " Yakushi.

297 _____.
Kanchenjunga, the untrodden peak/ by Charles
Evans. - 187 p. : ill. , maps.
"An account of the first ascent of Kanchenjunga in
1955 by the British party. " Yakushi.

298 _____.
On climbing/ by Charles Evans. - London: Museum
Press, 1954. - 191 p. : ill. , plates, maps.
"Book on mountaineering techniques, including some
Himalayan travels in the Rolwaling and Khumba Himal
of 1953. " Yakushi.

299 EVANS, Joan
The Conways: a history of three generations/ by
Joan Evans. - London: Museum Press, 1966. - 308
p. : map.
"The three generations dealt with here are of Martin Conway, his father and his daughter. The book is
based on Martin Conway's diaries and papers. M. Conway was a great pioneer in the Karakorum, and explored
there in 1892. " Yakushi.

300 _____.
Time and chance: the story of Arthur Evans and
his forebears/ by Joan Evans. - London: 410 p. : plates.

301 EVE, Arthur Stewart
Life and work of John Tyndall/ by Prof. A. S. Eve
and C. H. Creasey; with a chapter on Tyndall as a
mountaineer by Lord Schuster. - London: Macmillan,
1945. - 403 p. : plates.

302 [no entry]

303   EWBANK, John M.
      Rock climbs in the Blue Mountains/ by John Ew-
bank. - Sydney, N. S. W. : the Author, 1964. - 70 p. : ill.

304   FARQUHAR, Francis Peloubet
      First ascents in the United States, 1642-1900/ by
Francis P. Farquhar. - Berkeley, California: Grabhorn Press, 1948. - 12 p.
      "Presented to members of the American Alpine Club
at a meeting of the Sierra Nevada section in Berkeley. "
Dawson's.

305   _____ .
      A list of publications relating to the mountains of
Alaska/ by Francis P. Farquhar and Mildred P. Ashley. - New York: American Alpine Club, 1934. - 37 p.
      A very detailed list that includes newspaper and
magazine articles which completely describe this area
to 1934. Ed.

300   _____ .
      The literature of mountaineering/ by Francis P.
Farquhar. - Boston: Appalachian Mountain Club,
1940. - 39 p. : plates, ports.
      Reprinted from Appalachia, December, 1939 and
June, 1940.

307   FARRAR, John Percy
      The first ascent of the Finsteraarhorn/ by John P.
Farrar. - London: 1913.

308   _____ .
      On ropes and knots/ ed. by J. P. Farrar. - Pri-
vately printed, 1913.   8 p. : ill.

309   _____ .
      Some mountain expeditions of the Parkers/ by J.
Farrar. - London: 1916.

310   FEDDEN, R.
      The Enchanted Mountains/ by R. Fedden. - London:
Murray, 1962. - 124 p. : 9 plates, map.
      "Climbing holidays in the Val d'Aran Pyrenees. "
NBL.

311   FEDERATED MOUNTAIN CLUBS OF NEW ZEALAND
      Basic instruction manual/ by Federated Mountain

Clubs of Zealand. - Wellington: 32 p. : ill

312 _____ .
Safety in the mountains: a handbook for trampers,
skiers, stalkers and mountaineers/ ed. by B. R. Mason. - 5th ed. - Wellington, N. Z. : the clubs, 1963. -
120 p. : ill.
A basic, practical introduction for persons intending
to venture into the mountains or off the beaten track. Ed.

313 FELLOWES, Peregrine Forbes Morant
First over Everest: the Houston Mount Everest expedition, 1933/ by P. F. M. Fellowes, L. V. Stewart
Blacker and others. - London: John Lane, 1933. -
279 p. : 57 ill. , diagr. , maps.

314 FELLOWS, Charles
Narrative of an ascent to the summit of Mont Blanc/
by Charles Fellows. - London: 1827.
"Typical of the 'terror school' of mountain writers--
lacks literary merit and advises against the sport. " RHB.

315 FENTON, C. L.
Mountains/ by C. L. Fenton and M. A. Fenton. -
Garden City, N. Y. : 1942. - 160 p.

FENTON, M. A. see FENTON, C. L. (315)

316 FERLET, René
Aconcagua: south face/ by René Ferlet; trans. from
the French by E. Noel Bowman. - London: Constable,
1956. - 209 p. : 17 plates, maps.

317 FIELD, Ernest K. , ed.
Mountain search and rescue operations/ ed. by E.
K. Field, prepared by F. D. McLaren and others. -
Grand Teton Natural History Association, 1960.

318 FILES, Muriel, comp.
Catalogue of the library/ comp. by Muriel Files. -
Lancaster: Fell and Rock Climbing Club of the Lake
District, in association with the University of Lancaster,
1972. - 81 p. : limited ed. of 300 copies.
The most comprehensive mountaineering bibliography
to date, professionally arranged and indexed: based on
the English Lake District. Thoroughly British with a
few foreign publications. Ed.

319   FILIPPI, Filippo de
        The ascent of Mt. Elias by Prince Luigi Amadeo di
Savoia, Duke of the Abruzzi/ by F. de Filippi, illus.
by V. Sella and trans. from the Italian by L. Villari. -
Westminster: Constable, 1900. - 240 p.
        "First big mountain expedition to Alaska and the as-
sault of the highest peak. " NBL.

320   _____.
        Italian expedition to the Himalayas, Karakoram and
Eastern Turkestan, 1913-1914/ by F. de Filippi with
chapters by G. Danielli and J. A. Spranger; trans. from
the Italian by H. T. Lowe-porter, with an additional
chapter on the scientific results. - London: Edward
Arnold, 1932. - 528 p. : 5 panoramas, 300 ill. , 4 maps.

321   _____.
        Karakorum and the Western Himalayas 1909: an ac-
count of the expedition of Prince Luigi Amadeo of Savoy,
Duke of Abruzzi/ by F. de Filippi, with a preface by
the Duke of Abruzzi; trans. by Caroline Filippi and H.
T. Porter. London: Constable, 1912. 469 p. : panoramas, 16 plates, ill. , separate vol. of 18 plates and
maps plus index to text.
        "The full account of the ... expedition to K2 in the
Karakorum in 1909. " Yakushi.

322   _____.
        Ruwenzori: an account of the expedition by Prince
Luigi Amadeo of Savoy, Duke of the Abruzzi/ by F. de
Filippi; trans. from the Italian by Caroline de Filippi. -
London: Constable, 1908. - 408 p. : ill. , maps.

323   FINCH, George Ingle
        Climbing Mount Everest, etc. / by G. I. Finch. -
London: Philip, 1930. - 72 p. : (Philips' "New Pros-
pect" Readers)

324   _____.
        The making of a mountaineer/ by George Ingle
Finch. - London: Arrowsmith, 1924. - 340 p. : plates.
        "The author's mountaineering in the Alps, including
an account of the 1922 Mount Everest expedition. " Yakushi.   'Well written and unembroidered, the most thrilling experiences he describes simply. " RHB.

325   FIRSOFF, Valdemar Axel
        The Cairngorms on foot and ski: illus. by author. -

London: Hale, 1949. - 279 p. : plates, map.

326 _____.
Tatra mountains/ by V. A. Firsoff. - London:
Lindsay Drummond, 1942.

326a _____.
Arran with camera and sketchbook/ by V. A. Firsoff.

327 FITZGERALD, Edward Arthur
Climbs in the New Zealand Alps: being an account
of travel and discovery/ by E. A. Fitzgerald; with contributions by Sir M. Conway, Prof. T. G. Bonney. -
London: Fisher Unwin, 1896. - 363 p. : ill. , plates,
map.
"The first comprehensive book on the Southern Alps,
based on expeditions in 1894-5, including an ascent of
Mount Cook. " NBL.

328 _____.
The highest Andes: an account of the first ascent
of Aconagua and Tupungato in Argentina, and the exploration of the surrounding valleys/ by E. A. Fitzgerald,
with chapters by Stuart Vines and contributions by Prof.
Bonney and others. - London: Methuen, 1899. - 390 p. :
52 ill. , 2 maps, plates.
"Because of the highly coloured adjectives used, one
is less impressed than he would otherwise be. Less interesting than his previous book. " RHB.

329 FITZGIBBON, Mary Rose, ed.
Lakeland scene: articles from the Journal of the
Fell and Rock Climbing Club/ ed. by Mary Rose Fitz-
gibbon. - London: Chapman & Hall, 1948. - 240 p.

330 FORBES, James David
The tour of Mont Blanc and Monte Rosa: abridged
from the author's Travels in the Alps of Savoy/ by Dr.
James David Forbes. - Edinburgh: 1855.
"Dr. Forbes' books stimulated English climbers be-
fore the formation of the Alpine Club. Lucid, precise
yet pleasant style blending science and mountaineering."
RHB.

331 _____.
Travels through the Alps/ by J. D. Forbes. -

New ed. / rev. and annotated by W. A. B. Coolidge. -
London: Black, 1900. - 572 p. : maps.
Contents: travels through the Alps of Savoy; Journals of excursions; Pedestrianism in Switzerland; Topo-
graphy of the chain of Mont Blanc.

332 _____.
Travels through the Alps of Savoy, 1843 and other
parts of the Penine chain/ by James Forbes. - Edinburgh: 1845.
"Forbes' journeys of observation, mainly in the
Mont Blanc range, on which he based his theory of glaciers. Mt. Blanc, passage of the Col du Geant, Evo-
lena to Zermatt, tour of Mt. Rosa. " NBL.

333 FORTESQUE, Einifred
Mountain madness/ by Einifred Fortesque. - 1944. -
176 p. : ill.

334 FRANCIS, Godfrey H.
Mountain climbing/ by Godfrey II. Francis, with
diagrams by Erik Thorn. - 2nd ed. - London: English
University Press, 1964. - 192 p. : ill. , 8 plates, tables,
bibl. (Teach yourself books)
First pub. 1958. Covers the complete range of
rock climbing and therefore is brief on detail, with a
style that is more narrative than instructive. The first
edition was outdated in technique, i. e. it favored nailed
boots and was against the use of pitons; neither viewpoint obtains in the Second edition. Ed.

335 FRANCO, Jean
At grips with Jannu/ by J. Franco and Lionel Terray; preface by Lucien Davies and trans. from the
French by Hugh Merrick. - London: Gollancz, 1967. -
192 p. : 46 plates, maps, diagrs, 21 1/2cm.
A detailed account of an expedition with an interest
in people and places along the way as well as the actual ascent. Ed.

336 _____.
Makalu, 8470 metres (27,790 feet): the highest peak
yet conquered by an entire team/ by Jean Franco; trans.
from the French by Denise Morin. - London: Jonathan
Cape, 1957. - 256 p. : ill. , plates, maps, 20cm.
First pub. Paris: Arthaud, 1955. "The account of
the French Makalu expedition of 1955. They accomplish-

ed the 1st ascent of the summit by all members. " Yakushi.

337   FRASER, Colin
         The avalanche enigma/ by Colin Fraser. - London:
      Murray, 1966. - 301 p.: ill. , 26 plates, map, bibl.

338   FRASER, James Baillie
         Journal of a tour through part of the snowy range
      of the Himala Mountains, and to the sources of the ri-
      vers Jumna and Ganges/ by James Baillie Fraser. -
      London, 1920.

339   _____.
         Views of the Himala Mountains/ by James Baillie
      Fraser. - London: 1820. - col. plates, no text.

340   FREEMAN, Lewis R.
         On the roof of the Rockies: the great Columbia ice-
      field of the Canadian Rockies/ by Lewis R. Freeman. -
      London: Heinemann, 1926. - 270 p.: ill.

340a FREMONT, John Charles
         Report of an exploring expedition to the Rocky Moun-
      tains in the year 1842, and to Oregon and California in
      the years 1843-44/ by John Charles Fremont. - Wash-
      ington, D. C.:   1845. - maps, plates.

341   FRERE, Richard Burchmor
         Rock climbs/ by R. Frere. - 1938.

342   _____.
         Thoughts of a mountaineer/ by Richard Frere. -
      Edinburgh: Oliver and Boyd, 1952. - 177 p.: plates.

343   FRESHFIELD, Douglas William
         Below the snowline/ by D. W. Freshfield. - New
      York: 1923.
         "Greatest literary value of all the author's books:
      reprints some of his best articles on wanderings in
      mountain lands. " RHB.

344   _____.
         Exploration of the Caucasus/ by Douglas Freshfield;
      illus. , by V. Sella. - London: Edward Arnold, 1896.
         "Planned as a sort of Caucasian Peaks, Passes and
      Glaciers, with contributions by a number of climbers.

Still the most extensive work in English on the region."
NBL.

345   .
Italian Alps: sketches in the mountains of Ticino,
Lombardy, the Trentino and Venetia/ by Douglas Freshfield. - London: 1875. - 246 p. : plates.
'Impressions of a climber to whom mountains were
only one element in a region whose churches, villages
and unfrequented valleys he sensitively describes. " NBL.

346   .
The life of Horace Benedict de Saussure/ by Douglas Freshfield. - London: Arnold, 1920. - 479 p. :
plates.
"The life of the scientist who was determined that
Mont Blanc should be climbed, who offered a reward to
the first man up, and who led the second party to reach
the top in 1787. " NBL.

347   .
Round Kanchenjunga: a narrative of mountain travel
and exploration/ by D. W. Freshfield. - London: Edward Arnold, 1903. - 373 p. : ill. , map.
"A large volume dealing with an expedition to the
area surrounding the third highest mountain in the
world. " RHB.

348   .
Travels in the Central Caucasus and Bashan, including visits to Ararat and Tabreez and ascents of Ka-
zbek and Elbruz/ by D. W. Freshfield. - London: 1869.
"Gives a good account of the first ascents of the
ascents of Kasbek and Elbruz where the author had a
sensational experience with a crevasse. " RHB.

349   FRESHFIELD, (Mrs.) Henry
A summer tour in the Grisons and Italian Valleys
of the Bernina/ by Mrs. Henry Freshfield. - London:
1962. - 292 p. : 4 ill. , 2 maps.

350   FRISON-ROCHE, Roger
Mont Blanc and the seven valleys/ by R. Frison-
Roche and Pierre Tairraz; trans. from the French and
adapted by Roland le Grand with the co-operation of
Wilfred Noyce. - London: Kaye and Ward, 1961. -
267 p. : ill.

351 FRITH, Henry
    Ascents and adventures: a record of hardy moun-
taineering in every quarter of the globe/ by Henry
Frith. - London: Routledge & Kegan Paul, 1884. - 320
p. : ill.

    FROST, Tom see CHOUINARD (177)

352 FRYXELL, Fritiof Melvin
    The Teton peaks and their ascents/ by F. Fryxell. -
Grand Teton National Park, Wy. , The Grandall Studios,
1932. - 105 p. : plates, ill. , maps.
    "This account was written upon invitation of the Pub-
lication committee of the Appalachian Mountain Club and
was pub. serially in 'Appalachia'. " NUC. LC.

    GANSSER, August see HEIM, Arnold (425)

    GARDINER, Frederick see COOLIDGE, William Aug-
        ustus Brevoort (221)

353 GARDINER, John D.
    Ascent and tour of Mont Blanc and passage of the
Col du Geant, between Sept. 2nd and 7th, 1850/ by John
D. Gardiner. - Chiswick: 1851.

354 GARDNER, Arthur
    The art and sport of Alpine photography/ by Arthur
Gardner. - London: Witherby, 1927. - 224 p. : 150
plates.

    GARWOOD, Edmund J. see SELLA, Vittorio (853)

355 GASGUET, Francis Aidan
    His Holiness, Pope Pius XI: a pen portrait, and
The pope as Alpine Climber/ trans. from an article
written by himself. - London: Daniel O'Connor, 1922. -
30 p. : 28 ill. , port.

355a GAY, A. C.
    Some notes on mountaineering in the high Atlas/ by
A. C. Gay. - the Author, 1968. - 17 p.

356 GEIGER, H.
    Geiger and the Alps/ by H. Geiger. - Lucerne:
Oscar Bücher, 1966.

357 GEIST, Ronald C.
    Hiking, camping and mountaineering/ by Ronald

C. Geist. - New York: Harper, 1943. - 304 p. : ill. ,
plates, maps, diagr. , bibl.

GENTIL, P. F. <u>see</u> BURNS, W. C. (149a)

358 GEORGE, Hereford Brooke
Munchausen on the Jungfrau / by H. B. George and
C. E. Mathews. - London: [n. d.]. - Fiction.

359 _____ .
The Oberland and its glaciers: explored and illus-
trated with ice-axe and camera / by Hereford Brooks
George. - with twenty-eight photographic illus. by E.
E. Edwards, and a map of the Oberland. - London:
1866.

GEORGES, Joseph <u>see</u> THOMPSON, Dorothy Evelyn (974)

360 GERVASUTTI, Giusto
Gervasutti's climbs / by G. Gervasutti; trans. from
the Italian by Nea Morin and Janet Adam Smith. - London: Hart Davis, 1957. - 201 p. : 14 plates.
Orig. pub. as Scalate nelle Alpi, 1947.

361 GESNER, Conrad
On the admiration of mountains: the prefatory letter addressed to Jacob Avienus ... etc. / by Conrad
Gesner, ed. by W. Dock. - San Francisco: Grabhorn
Press, 1937. - 54 p. : ill.
Contents: A description of the Riven Mountain,
commonly called Mount Pilatus / by Conrad Gesner
(1555), trans. by H. B. D. Soule; and, On Conrad Gesner and the mountaineering of Theurdank / by J. Monroe Thorington, with bibliographical notes by W. Dock
and J. Monroe Thorington.

362 GILBERT, Josiah
The Dolomite mountains: excursions through Tyrol,
Corinthia, Corniola and Friuli in 1861, 1862, 1863; with
a geological chapter and pictorial illustrations from
original drawings on the spot / by J. Gilbert and G. C.
Churchill. - London: 1864.
"First English description of this mountain district,
but from the point of view of the carriage traveller, who
frequently deserted the roads for mountain tracks. " NBL.

363 _____ .
Six letters relating to travel, 1865-69 / by Josiah

Gilbert. - n. p. : privately printed, 1954. - 41 p.

364 GILKINSON, W. Scott
Aspiring, New Zealand: the romantic story of the Matterhorn of the southern Alps/ by W. Scott Gilkinson. - n. p. : privately printed, 1961. - 80 p. : ill.

365 GILL, Michael
Mountain midsummer: climbing in four continents/ by Michael Gill. - London: Hodder and Stoughton, 1969. - 220 p. : 48 ill. , maps.
"Climbing autobiography by a young New Zealander, including the Himalayan expeditions led by E. Hillary; to Ama Dablam and Makalu in 1960-61, and to Kangtega in 1963. " Yakushi.

366 GILLMAN, Peter
Eiger direct = Direttissima/ by P. Gillman and Dougal Haston; photographs by Chris Bonington. - London: Collins, 1966. - 183 p. : 40 plates (15 col.)
A modern sequel to the White Spider showing the peak of modern ice climbing by Dougal Haston plus the artificial techniques of Layton Kor under the siege management of the late John Harlin. An epic. Ed.

367 GILLY, William Stephens
Narrative of an excursion to the mountains of Piedmont, with maps, plates, and an appendix, containing copies of ancient manuscripts/ by William Stephens Gilly. - 3rd ed. - London: 1826.
First pub. 1824.

368 GIRDLESTONE, Arthur Gilbert
The high Alps without guides: being a narrative of adventures in Switzerland, together with chapters on the practicability of such mode of mountaineering/ by A. G. Girdlestone. - London: 1870.
"Greatly popular in its day, but more for its delightful spirit of adventure than its literary quality. " RHB.

GOOLD-ADAMS, H. E. see CAVENDISH, Alfred Edward John (164)

369 GORDON, S. P.
The charm of the hills/ S. P. Gordon. - London: Cassell, 1912. - 248 p.

369a GOS, Charles
Alpine tragedy/ by C. Gos; trans. by Malcolm
Barnes. - London: Allen & Unwin, 1948. - 282 p. :
plates.
The Matterhorn disaster of Whymper's first success-
ful attempt. Ed.

370 GOS, François Marc Eugene
Rambles in high Savoy/ by François Gos; trans.
by Frank Kemp. - London: Longmans, 1928. - 169 p. :
ill.
"Well written descriptions of walks and minor
climbs which recreates for the armchair mountaineer
some of the scenes and moods of the Alps. " BRD.

371   .
‾‾‾‾‾‾Zermatt and its valley/ by François Gos. - London:
Cassell, 1926. - 180 p. : ill.

372 GOSWAMI, S. M.
Everest: is it conquered?/ by S. M. Goswami. -
Calcutta: Indian Press, 1954. - 122 p.
"The author claims that the British expedition of
1953 did not ascend Mount Everest!" Yakushi.

373 GRAHAM, F. , ed.
Recent developments on gritsone/ by members of
the Rucksack Club, Yorkshire Ramblers' Club and Grit-
sone Club; ed. by F. Graham.

374 GRAHAM, J. D.
Rock climbing in Malta/ by J. D. Graham. - Reading, West Col Productions, 1971. - 103 p. : ill. , map,
index.

GRAHAM, Peter see HEWITT, H. B. (430)

375 GRAHAM, W. W.
Climbing the Himalayas/ by W. W. Graham. -
London: Isbister, 1887.
"The author, with Swiss guides, made his explora-
tions and mountaineerings in the region of Kangchenjunga
and of the Garhwal in 1883. He claimed he ascended
Changabang (A-21), Jobonu, and Kabru, but it is very
doubtful. " Yakushi.

376 GRANT, Richard Henry
Annapurna II/ by Richard Henry Grant. - London·

Kimber, 1961. - 192 p. : 8 plates, maps.

377   GRAY, A.
       A big grey man of Ben Macdhui / by A. Gray. -
       Aberdeen: Impulse Books, 1970.

378   GRAY, Dennis
       Rope boy / by Dennis Gray. - London: Gollancz,
       1970. - 320 p. : 31 plates, ill. , maps, ports.
       Biography of a man associated with the greats:
       Whillans, Brown, Nat Allen--a good modern approach
       to mountaineering in Britain, Alps, Himalayas and South
       America. Ed.

379   GREAT BRITAIN. Air Department
       Mountain rescue: training handbook for Royal Air
       Force mountain rescue teams. - 2nd ed. - London:
       H. M. S. O. , 1968. - 178 p. : ill. , forms. (PAM Air 299)
       A very basic rock-climbing manual meant for be-
       ginners. Has only one chapter on rescue, poor by com-
       parison to Mariner or McInnes. Ed.

380   GREEN, William Spotswood
       Among the Selkirk Glaciers: being an account of a
       survey in the Rocky Mountain regions of British Colum-
       bia / by William Spotswood Green. - London: Macmillan,
       1890. - 251 p. : ill. , map.

381   _____.
       The high alps of New Zealand: or, a trip to the
       glaciers of the Antipodes with an ascent of Mount Cook /
       by William Spotswood Green. - London: Macmillan,
       1883. - 350 p.

382   _____.
       Report on a journey among the New Zealand gla-
       ciers in 1882 / by William Spotswood Green. - Dublin:
       1882.

383   GREENBANK, Anthony
       Instructions in rock climbing / by Anthony Green-
       back. - London: Museum Press, 1963. - 159 p. : ill. ,
       diagr. , 8 plates (Brompton library)
       A book for the young beginner, deliberately excludes
       detailed and advanced technique. Possibly oversimpli-
       fied in that it is also meant for non-climbers. Ed.

383a GREENE, Raymond
Moments of being: the random recollections of Raymond Greene. - London: Heinemann, 1974.

384 _____ .
Oxford and Cambridge mountaineering, 1921/ by Raymond Greene. - London: Cambridge University Press, 1921.

385 GREGORY, Alfred, ed.
The picture of Everest: a book of full color reproductions of photographs of the Everest scene/ chosen and explained by A. Gregory. - London: Hodder and Stoughton, 1954.
Selected from the pictures taken by members of the British Mount Everest Expedition, 1953. Ed.

386 GRIBBLE, Francis
The early mountaineers/ by Francis Gribble. - London: Allen and Unwin, 1899. - 338 p. : ill.

387 _____ .
The story of alpine climbing/ by Francis Gribble. - London: George Newnes, 1903. (Library of useful stories)

388 GROHMAN, William Adolph Baillie
Camps in the Rockies: being a narrative of life on the frontier and sport in the Rocky Mountains/ by W. A. B. Grohman. - London: Sampson Low, 1882. - 438 p. : ill. , map.

389 _____ .
Sport in the Alps in the past and present ... with ... some sporting reminiscences of ... the late Duke (Ernest) of Saxe-Coburg-Gotha/ by W. A. B. Grohman. - London: Black, 1896. - 356 p. : ill.

390 _____ .
Tyrol and the Tyrolese: the people and the land in their social, sporting and mountaineering aspects ... with illustrations/ by W. A. B. Grohman. - London: 1876.

391 GURUNG, Harka Bahadur
Annapurna to Dhaulagiri: a decade of mountaineering in Nepal Himalaya, 1950-1960/ by G. Harka. -

Nepal: Department of Information, 1968.
"A short history of mountaineering in the Nepal
Himalaya. " Yakushi.

392 GYAN, Singh
Lure of Everest: story of the first Indian expedi-
tion/ by Singh Gyan; with a foreword by Jawaharlal
Nehru. - Delhi: Ministry of Information and Broadcasting, 1961. - 212 p. : ill. , plates, maps, 21 1/2cm.
An interesting account of an attempt by the Indian
government to climb Everest. The operation was full
of national fervor to the extent of manufacturing their
own equipment and organizing the expedition along mili-
tary lines. Ed.

GYATSO, Sanam see MALLIK, B. N. (587)

393 HAGEN, Toni
Mount Everest: formation, population and exploration of the Everest region/ by T. Hagen and others;
trans. from the German by E. Noel Bowman. - London:
O. U. P. , 1963. - 195 p. : 24 plates, maps, tables, bibl.

394   .
Nepal: the kingdom in the Himalayas/ by Toni Hagen. - Chicago: 1971. - 180 p. : ill. , 24 col. & 42
monochrome plates, 24 maps.

395 HAINES, Aubrey
Mountain fever: historic conquests of Rainier/ by
Aubrey Haines. - Oregon Historical Society, 1973.

396 HALL, Richard Watson
The art of mountain tramping/ by Richard W. Hall. -
London: Witherby, 1932. - 191 p. : plates. (Sports and
pastimes library)

397   .
On Cumbrian Fells: papers on rockclimbing with
other pieces in prose and verse/ by Richard W. Hall. -
Whitehaven: Whitehaven News, 1926. - 76 p.

398   .
Some Cumbrian climbs and equipment/ by Richard
Watson Hall. - n. p. : privately printed, 1920's. - 35 p.

399 HAMER, A. Handel
The spell of the mountains/ by A. Handel Hamer. -

Port Elizabeth: Juta, 1917. - 74 p.

400 HAMER, Samuel H.
        The Dolomites/ by S. H. Hamer. - 2nd ed. -
London: Methuen, 1910. - 305 p. : ill.

401 HAMILTON, Helen
        Mountain madness/ by Helen Hamilton. - London:
Collins & Sons, 1922. - ix, 274 p.

402 HANKINSON, Alan
        The first tigers: the early history of rockclimbing
in the Lake District/ by Alan Hankinson. - London:
Dent, 1972. - 196 p. : 16 plates, ill. , ports. , bibl. ,
index.
        A detailed history of climbing in Britain pre 1900.
Very good character sketches but mainly of historical
interest. Ed.

403 HARDIE, Norman
        In highest Nepal: our life among the Sherpas/ by
Norman Hardie. - London: Allen & Unwin, 1957. -
191 p. : 16 ill. , maps.
        "The account of living with Sherpas in Solu-Khumba
after the successful British Kangchenjunga expedition of
1955. " Yakushi.

HARKA, Gurung Bahadur see GURUNG, Harka B. (391)

404 HARKER, George
        Easter climbs of the British Alpine Club/ by G.
Harker. - Sherrett & Hughes, 1913. - 141 p.

405 HARPER, Arthur P.
        Memories of mountains and men/ by Arthur P.
Harper. - Christchurch, N. Z. : Simpson & Williams,
1946.

406 _____.
        Pioneer work in the alps of New Zealand/ by Ar-
thur P. Harper. - London: Fisher Unwin, 1896. - 336
p. : maps, ill.
        20 copies on Japan paper in British Museum.

407 HARPER, Stephen
        Lady killer peak: a lone man's story of twelve wo-
men on a killer mountain/ by Stephen Harper. - London:
World Distributors, 1965. - 123 p. (Consul Books)

408   HARRER, Heinrich
        Seven years in Tibet/ by Heinrich Harrer. - Lon-
don: Hart-Davis, 1954. - 288 p. : ill.

409   _____ .
        The white spider: the history of the north face of
the Eiger/ by Heinrich Harrer; trans. from the German
by Hugh Merrick. - London: Hart Davis, 1959. - 240
p. : ill. , plates.
        Extremely interesting history of attempts to climb
the greatest technical problem in mountaineering. The
fascination for this particular North Face is well com-
municated. Ed.

410   HARRIS, George W.
        A land apart: the Mount Cook alpine region/ by G.
Harris and Graeme Hosler. - Wellington, N. Z. :   Reed,
1971. - 224 p. : ill.

411   HARRIS, Walter B.
        Tafilet: the narrative of a journey of exploration
in the Atlas Mountains and the oasis of the N. W. Saha-
ra/ by Walter T. Harris; illus. by Maurice Romberg. -
London: Blackwood, 1895. - 386 p. : ill. , maps.
        "Contains long chapters on the ascent of the Atlas,
the mountains and the Berbers and the descent of the
Atlas. " Campbell (see entry 157).

412   HARRISON, Frederic
        My Alpine Jubilee, 1851-1907/ by Frederic Harri-
son. - London: Smith, Elder, 1908. - 141 p.

413   HART, John L. Jerome
        Fourteen thousand feet: a history of the naming
and early ascents of the high Colorado peaks/ by John
L. J. Hart. - Denver: Colorado Mountain Club, 1925. -
51 p. : map.

414   HASTON, Dougal
        In high places/ by D. Haston. - London: Cassell,
1972. - 168 p. : 16 plates, ill.
        See also GILLMAN, Peter (366)

415   HAUSER, Gunther
        White mountain and tawny plain/ by Gunther Hauser;
trans. from the German by Richard Rickett. - London:
Allen & Unwin, 1961. - 224 p. : front. , 3 maps, plates.

Orig. pub. as Ihr herren Berge, 1959.

416 HAWES, William
Narrative of an ascent to the summit of Mont Blanc
made during the summer of 1827 by Mr. W. Hawes and
Mr. C. (Sir Charles) Fellows, including a letter written
by Mr. W. Hawes on the top of Mont Blanc. - the Author, 1820.

417 HAYDEN, Sir Henry Hubert
Sport and travel in the highlands of Tibet / by Sir
H. H. Hayden and Cesar Casson, etc. - London: Rich-
ard Cobden-Sanderson, 1927. - 262 p. : plates, map.

418 HAZARD, Joseph T.
Pacific crest trails from Alaska to Cape Horn / by
Joseph T. Hazard. - Seattle.

419 _____.
Snow sentinels of the Pacific Northwest / by Joseph
T. Hazard. - Seattle: 1932. - 249 p. : 32 ill.
"History of Mount Olympus, Garibaldi, Baker, Gla-
cier Peak, Rainier, St. Helens, Adams and Hood."
Dawson's.

420 HEADLEY, Joel Tyler, ed.
Mountain adventures in various parts of the world:
selected from the narratives of celebrated travellers /
ed. with an intro. and additions by J. T. Headley. -
New York: Scribner, 1872. - 356 p. : 41 ill. , plates.

421 _____.
Travels in Italy, the Alps and the Rhine / by J. T.
Headley. - Dublin: J. M'Glashan, 1849. - 350 p.

422 HECKEL, Vilem
Climbing in the Caucasus by V. Heckel / text by
Josef Styrsa; foreword by Sir John Hunt and trans. by
Till Gottheiner. - London: Spring Books, 1958? - 207
p. : chiefly ill. , 28cm.

423 HEDERATUS, pseud
Cambridge night climbing / by Hederatus. - London:
Chatto and Windus, 1970. - 95 p. : 32 plates, ill.
Unorthodox climbs in the Cambridge college with
flash photographs; an interesting variation of a sport.
Ed.

424 HEDIN, Sven
   Trans-Himalaya: discoveries and adventures in Ti-
bet/ by Sven Hedin. - London: Macmillan, 1909. -
2 vols. , ill. , maps.
   A story of travel with scientific observations, but
little climbing. Interesting narrative of this Swedish
Expedition. Ed.

425 HEIM, Arnold
   The throne of the gods: an account of the first
Swiss expedition to the Himalaya/ by Arnold Heim and
August Gansser. - London: Macmillan, 1939. - 233 p. :
ill.

425a HEINE, A. J.
   Mountaincraft manual/ by A. J. Heine. - Welling-
ton, N. Z. : National Mountains Safety Council of New
Zealand, 1971. - 170 p. : ill.
   Cover title: Mountaincraft: your basic manual.
A basic but comprehensive and concise manual with
specific sections on New Zealand conditions. Ed.

426 HENDERSON, Kenneth Atwood
   Manual of American mountaineering/ by Kenneth
Atwood Henderson. - New York: American Alpine Club,
1941. - 179 p. : 3 plates, tables.
   Also pub. as The American Alpine Club's Handbook
of American Mountaineering (Boston: Houghton Miflin,
1942). "An extremely detailed and clearly printed manual especially for American conditions prepared for
training U. S. Army mountain troops. " BRD.

427 HERFORD, Siegfried Wedgwood
   In memoriam Siegfried Wedgwood Herford. - n. p. :
privately printed, 1916?
   Obituary notices by various authors. Ed.

428 HERRIGKOFFER, Karl M.
   Nanga Parbat: incorporating the official report of
the Austro-German expedition of 1953/ by Karl M. Herrigkoffer; trans. with additional information by Eleanor
Brockett and Anton Ehrenzweig. - London: Elek Books,
1954. - 208 p. : 8 plates, maps. Rev. ed. by Hamilton,
1956. (Panther Books)
   "Summarises the previous attempts ... tells the
story of Hermann Buhl, who reached the top by himself."
NBL.

429   HERZOG, Maurice
        Annapurna: conquest of the first 8,000 metre peak
      (26,493 feet)/ by Maurice Herzog; trans. from the
      French by Nea Morin and Janet Adam Smith. - London:
      Reprint Society, 1954. - 254 p. : ill. , 8 plates.
        "A French expedition's success and ordeal by ...
      avalanche on the first peak over 8,000 metres. " NBL.
        See also KENNETT, John (496)

430   HEWITT, H. B. , ed.
        Peter Graham: mountain guide; an autobiography/
      ed. by H. B. Hewitt, foreword and epilogue by John
      Pascoe. - Wellington, N. Z. : Reed, 1965. - 245 p. : ill.

430a HEWITT, L. Rodney
        Mount Cook alpine regions/ by L. R. Hewitt and
      M. Davidson. - 2nd rev. ed. - Christchurch, N. Z. :
      Pegasus Press, 1972. - 72 p. : plates.
        Virtually a guide book, but also contains details of
      climbers and of this area. Ed.

431   ────── .
        Mountains of New Zealand/ by R. Hewitt and Mavis
      Davidson. - Wellington, N. Z. : Reed, 1954. - 127 p. :
      ill.

432   HIEBLER, Tony
        North face in winter: the first winter climb of the
      Eiger's north face, March, 1961/ by Tony Hiebler;
      trans. by Hugh Merrick. - London: Barrie and Rock-
      liff, 1962. - 121 p. : 14 plates.

433   HILLARY, Sir Edmund Percival
        East of Everest: New Zealand Alpine Club Himala-
      an expedition to the Barun Valley in 1954/ by Sir E.
      Hillary and George Love. - London: Hodder and Stough
      ton, 1956. - 71 p. : 48 plates, 3 maps.

434   ────── .
        High adventure/ by Sir Edmund Hillary. - London:
      Hodder and Stoughton, 1955. - 224 p. : 31 plates, maps. ,
      ill.
        With maps by A. Spark and sketches by George
      Djurkavic. An account of the author's mountaineering
      experiences with special references to the 1953 Mount
      Everest Expedition. Ed.

435

      <u>   </u>.
    High in the thin cold air / by Sir Edmund Hillary
and Desmond Doig. - London: Hodder and Stoughton,
1963. - 287 p. : 32 plates, maps, 21 1/2cm.
    Part 1, In search of snowmen, by Desmond Doig.
Part 2, Our Life in the clouds, by E. Hillary.

436

      <u>   </u>.
    No latitude for error / by Sir Edmund Hillary. -
London: Hodder and Stoughton, 1961. - 225 p. : front. ,
plates, ports. , maps, tables.
    Antarctica.

437

      <u>   </u>.
    Schoolhouse in the clouds / by Sir Edmund Hillary. -
London: Hodder and Stoughton, 1965. - Harmondsworth:
Penguin Books, 1968. - (Penguin) 192 p. : 8 plates, ill. ,
ports.
    Book on the Sherpas, includes an ascent of Kange-
tega and Taweche.
    See also MOON, Kenneth William (640); HUNT, Sir
Henry Cecil John (466); and KNOOP, Faith Yingling (505)

438 HIMALAYAN CLUB
    A climber's guide to Sanamang, Kashmir. - New
Delhi: Himalayan Club, 1945. - 51 p. : ill. , map.

439 HINCHLIFF, Thomas Woodbine
    Summer months in the Alps: with the ascent of
Monte Rosa / by Thomas W. Hinchliff. - London: 1857.
    "Fresh and charming account, continually in good
spirits in contrast with earlier accounts. " RHB.

440 HINDLEY, Geoffrey
    The roof of the world / by Geoffrey Hindley. - Lon-
don: Aldus, 1971. - 191 p. : ill. , col. facsims. , maps,
ports. (Aldus encyclopaedia of discovery and exploration)

441 HIRST, John, comp.
    The songs of the mountaineers / collected and ed.
by J. Hirst. - Manchester: Rucksack Club, 1922.

442 HOARE, Robert John
    The high peaks / by R. J. Hoare; illus. by Carlo
Alexander. - London: Ginn, 1966. - 80 p. : ill. , maps,
diagr. , bibl. (Modern age readers, no. 5)

443 HODGKIN, Robert Allason
     Reconnaissance on an educational frontier / by Ro-
     bert Allason Hodgkin. - London: Oxford University
     Press, 1970. - 108 p. : ill. , bibl.

444 HOHLE, Per
     Mountain world of Norway / by Per Hohle; trans.
     from the Norwegian by Ragnar Christophersen. - Oslo:
     Dreyer, 1956. - 104 p. : ill.

445 HOLMES, Peter
     Mountains and a monastry / by Peter Holmes. -
     London: Geoffrey Bles, 1958. - 191 p. : 8 plates, 2
     maps.
     "The author visited Spiti in India both in 1955 and
     in 1956, but it is only with the second of these trips
     that this account is concerned. They climbed a number
     of new peaks around the 20,000 feet mark at the head
     of the Ratang Nulla. " Yakushi.

446 HOLMES, William Kersly
     On Scottish hills / by W. K. Holmes. - Rev. ed. -
     Edinburgh: Oliver and Boyd, 1962. - 128 p. : front. ,
     15 plates.
     Orig. pub. as Tramping the Scottish hills, 1946.

     HOLWAY, Edward W. D. see PALMER, Howard (729)

447 HOLWORTHY, Sophia Matilda
     Alpine scrambles and classic rambles: a gipsy tour
     in search of summer snow and winter sun / by the author
     of Scylla and Charybdis. - London: J. Nisbet and Co. ,
     1855. - 114 p.

448 HOOKER, Sir Joseph D.
     Himalayan Journals / by Sir Joseph Hooker. - 2
     vols. - London: 1854.

449 HORIZON (New York)
     Mountain conquest / by the ed. of Horizon magazine;
     text by Eric Shipton in consultation with Bradford Wash-
     burn. - London: Cassell, 1967. - 153 p. : chiefly ill. ,
     maps, facsims. (Caravel book, no. 19)
     An essential book combining all historical and pic-
     torial history of mountaineering. The pages are illustra-
     ted by photographs, many in color with informative text.
     Ed.

450 HORNBEIN, Thomas Frederick
Everest--west ridge/ by Thomas F. Hornbein. -
London: Allen & Unwin, 1971. - 181 p.: ill., 15 plates.
First pub. San Francisco: Sierra Club, 1965. "An
account of the Everest west ridge climbing by the Amer-
ican expedition of 1963. " Yakushi.

451 HORNBY, Emily
Mountaineering records/ by E. H. (comp. by M.
L. Hornby). - Liverpool: Thompson, 1907. - 352 p.

HOSLER, Graeme see HARRIS, George W. (410)

452 HOSMER, J. K.
History of the expeditions of captains Lewis and
Clark, 1804-5-6/ by J. K. Hosmer.

453 HOUSTON, Charles Sneed
The American Karakoram Expedition to K2, 1938/
by Charles S. Houston.

454 _____.
K2, the savage mountain/ by C. Houston and other
members of the Third American Karakoram Expedition;
maps and line drawing by Clarence Doore. - London:
Collins, 1955. - 192 p.: ill., maps, plates.
"A recommended simple and very emotional account
of the ordeal of an unsuccessful expedition. " BRD.

455 HOWARD, Eliot, ed.
A pioneer in the high Alps: alpine diaries and letters of F. F. Tuckett, 1856-1874/ ed. by Eliot Howard
and W. A. B. Coolidge. - London: Edward Arnold,
1920. - 372 p.: ill., ports.
"Literary ability not as great as his friend Leslie
Stephen, the author is less writer than climber, but
under stress of emotion writes graphically. " RHB.

456 HOWARD, Tony
Walks and climbs in Romsdal, Norway/ by Tony
Howard. - Manchester: Ciarare Press, 1970. - 170 p.:
ill., maps.

457 HOWARD, William D.
Photographs among the Dolomite mountains/ by W.
D. Howard and F. H. Lloyd, 1865.

458 _____ .
    Narrative of a journey to the summit of Mont Blanc, made in July, 1819/ Baltimore: 1821.

459 HOWARD-BURY, Charles Kenneth
    Mount Everest--the reconnaissance/ by C. K. Howard-Bury. - London: Edward Arnold, 1921. - 356 p.: ill., maps, plates.
    The first expedition into this uncharted wilderness. It is well illustrated, though the text is a little too factual, relieved in part by Mallory's account of the attack on Everest. Ed.

460 HUDSON, Charles
    Where there's a will, there's a way: an ascent of Mt. Blanc by a new route and without guides/ by C. Hudson and Edward Shirley Kennedy. - 2nd ed. - London: Longmans, 1856.
    "Record of the first guideless ascent of Mt. Blanc by a group of young Englishmen. 2nd edition describes 2 ascents of Mont Rosa. " NBL.

461 HUMBLE, Benjamin Hutchinson
    The Cullin of Skye/ by B. H. Humble. - London: 1952. - 144 p.: 73 ill.
    "The Cullin are a comparatively small range of mountains in one corner of the Isle of Skye which offers an exciting challenge to the enthusiastic rockclimber. " Dawson's.

462 _____ .
    On Scottish hills/ by B. H. Humble. - London: Chapman & Hall, 1946. - 128 p.: 75 plates.
    "From Turner, Scott and other early tourists to the latest experts. Reflects the social change in climbing over the last fifty years. " NBL.

463 [no entry]

464 HUNT, Sir Henry Cecil John
    Sir John Hunt's diary (Everest 1953), published in The Alpine Journal, vol. 59, no. 287, pages 123-172. 1953.

465 _____ .
    The ascent of Everest/ by Sir John Hunt, with a chapter on the final assault by Sir Edmund Hillary.

Foreword by H. R. H. the Duke of Edinburgh. - London:
Hodder & Stoughton, 1953. - 229 p. : ill., 48 plates.
Also pub. under title: Conquest of Everest. Simple, detailed, matter of fact report of the successful
ascent of Mount Everest. A definitive account worth
reading. Ed.

466 _____.
Our Everest adventure: the pictorial history from
Katmandu to the summit/ by Sir John Hunt. - Leicester:
Brockhampton Press, 1954. - 127 p. : chiefly plates.
"Largely told in pictures, with Hillary's own account
of the successful ascent." BRD. Based on the official
photographs of the expedition with a little journalistic
narrative. Ed.

467 _____.
The red snows: an account of the British Caucasus
Expedition, 1958/ by Sir John Hunt and Christopher
Brasher. - London: Hutchinsons, 1960. - 176 p. : 16
plates, map, 21cm.
"An interesting insight into Russian mountaineering
and of this seldom visited region which includes an ap-
pendix on the mountaineering history of the region. Ed.
See also WYMER, Norman George (1116)

468 HUNT, R. A.
White mountain holidays/ by R. A. Hunt.

469 HUXLEY, Anthony
Standard encyclopaedia of the world's mountains/ by
Anthony Huxley. - London: Weidenfeld & Nicholson,
1962. - 383 p. : ill., ports., 16 col. plates, maps.

470 INDIAN MOUNT EVEREST EXPEDITION, 1965
By the Armed Forces Information Officer. - New
Delhi: Minister of Defence on behalf of the Indian
Mountaineering Foundation, 1965. - 43 p. : ill.

470a INGRAM, J. A.
Fellcraft: some advice for fellwalkers/ by J. A.
Ingram.

471 IRVING, Robert Lock Graham
The Alps ... illustrated from photographs/ by R.
L. G. Irving. - 3rd ed. - London: Batsford, 1947. -
120 p.

First pub. 1939. "Main interest lies in the photography. Written for the general traveller, but is infused
by the author's interest in mountain climbing. " RBD.

472   .
        A history of British mountaineering/ by R. L. G.
Irving. - London: Batsford, 1955. - 240 p. : 65 ill. ,
plates.

473   .
        The Mountain way: an anthology in prose and verse/
collected by R. L. G. Irving. - London: Dent, 1938.
        "A more strictly climbing anthology than Lunn's The
Englishman in the Alps ... includes Petrarch on his ascent of Mont Ventoux in 1336. " NBL.

474   .
        Mountains shall bring peace/ by R. L. G. Irving. -
London: Blackwell, 1947. - 47 p.

475   .
        The romance of mountaineering/ by R. L. G. Irv-
ing. - London: Dent, 1935. - 320 p.
        "Historical survey with some personal chapters:
Mr. Irving introduced George Mallory, when a schoolboy,
to the Alps. " NBL.

476   .
        Ten great mountains, etc. / by R. L. G. Irving.
London: Dent, 1940. - 213 p. : ill. , plates.
        "Geographic, scenic description of 10 mountains plus
accounts of the most important ascent of each. Includes
Snowden, Mt. Cook, Matterhorn, Mont Blanc, Nanga
Parbat, Kanchenjunga and Mt. Everest. " BRD.

477   IRWIN, William Robert
        Challenge: an anthology of the literature of moun-
taineering/ by Robert Irwin. - New York: Columbia
University Press, 1950. - 444 p.
        "Shows mountaineering can be almost as fascinating
to read as murders. No photos, or mention of Mount
Everest, but worth reading. " BRD.

ISHERWOOD, Christopher see AUDEN, Wystan Hugh (35)

478   IZZARD, Ralph William Burdick
        The abominable snowman adventure/ by R. Izzard. -

London: Hodder & Stoughton, 1955. - 302 p. : 26 ill.,
plates.
"An account of the Daily Mail Himalayan Yeti expedition of 1954. The author organized the expedition
of nine members and spent four months in and around
Mamche Bazar, and the area about Everest." Yakushi.

479 ———.
The innocent on Everest/ by Ralph Izzard. - London: Hodder and Stoughton, 1955. - 255 p. : plates,
bibl.
A journalist's account of his assignment to unofficial-
ly cover the 1953 British Everest Expedition. Ed.

480 JACKSON, John A.
More than mountains/ by John A. Jackson. - London: Harrap, 1955. - 213 p. : ill., 4 maps, music,
47 plates, maps, 21 cm.
An attempt to popularize mountaineering and therefore not intended for climbers. Sensitively written with
due consideration for the flora and fauna and Yeti. Ed.
See also IZZARD, Ralph William Burdick (478)

481 JACKSON, M.
Tents in the clouds: the first Women's Himalayan
Expedition/ by M. Jackson and Elizabeth Stark. - Lon-
don: Collins, 1956. - 255 p. : 24 plates, 5 maps, 21 cm.
"An account of the Jugal Himal expedition in Nepal
of 1955. They ascended Gyaltsen Peak 6700 cm."
Yakushi.

482 ———.
The Turkish time machine/ by M. Jackson. - Lon-
don: Hodder & Stoughton, 1967.
The Cilo Dag mountains of Turkey. Ed.

483 JAMES, Ron
Rock climbing in Wales/ by Ron James. - London:
Constable, 1970. - 241 p. : ill., port.

484 ———.
Rock face: techniques of rock climbing/ by Ron
James. - London: British Broadcasting Corp., 1974. -
118 p. : ill., 20 cm.

485 JAPANESE ALPINE CLUB
Manaslu, 1954/ 56/ by Japanese Alpine Club. -

Tokyo: 1958. - 353 p. : ill. , plates, maps.
"Text in Japanese but illustrations have English captions and the introduction and some sections are translated into English. " Dawson's.

486 JAVELLE, Jean Marie Ferdinand Emile
Alpine memories: with a biographical and literary notice by Eugene Rambert/ by Emile Javelle trans. from the French and with an intro. by W. R. Chesson. - London: Unwin, 1899. - vii, 444 p.
Also pub. under title: Mountain memories

487 JEFFERS, Leroy
The call of the mountains: rambles among the mountains and canyons of the United States and Canada/ by Leroy Jeffers. - London: Fisher Unwin, 1923. - 282 p. : ill. , 100 plates.
"A charming and inspiring account with notable illustrations intended for the general reader as well as the dedicated climber. " BRD.

488 ─────
Selected list of books on mountaineering/ by Leroy Jeffers. - Rev. ed. - New York: New York Public Library, 1916. - 46 p. (New York Public Library. Lists of works on particular subjects)

489 JEGERLEHNER, Johannes
Alp legends/ collected by Johannes Jegerlehner, trans. by I. M. Whitworth. - Manchester: Sherratt & Hughes, 1926. - 206 p. : ill.

JERSTED, Lute see McCALLUM, J. D. (573)

490 JOHANNESBURG PUBLICITY DEPARTMENT
The challenge of the Drakensberg: the Mont aux sources group/ Johannesburg Publicity Department. - Johannesburg: the Department, n. d. - 35 p. : ill.

491 JOHNSON, Stowers
Mountains and no mules/ by Stowers Johnson. - London: Fortune Press, 1949. - 208 p.

492 JONES, Owen Glynne
Rockclimbing in the English Lake district/ by Owen Glynne Jones; with a memoir of the author by W. M. Crook and two appendices by George and Ashley Abra-

ham. - 2nd ed. - 1911.
First pub. London: Longmans, 1897. Facsim. reprint of 2nd ed. Manchester: Morten, 1973. "The first book to come from the enthusiasm of British climbers for the sport to be found in their own hills. "
NBL.

493 JONES, Trevor
Snowden south/ by T. Jones and John Neill; with a geological note by N. J. Soper, natural history notes by R. Goodier and diagrams by R. B. Evans. - 2nd ed. - London: Climbers' Club, 1966. - 150 p. : ill., maps, tables. (Climbers' Club guides to Wales, 8)

494 KAIN, Conrad, ed.
Where the clouds can go / ed. with additional chapters by J. Monroe Thorington. - New ed. - Boston: 1954. - 456 p. : plates.
First pub. New York: American Alpine Club, 1935. Mountaineering in Europe, Canada, New Zealand and Siberia. Ed.

495 KELLY, H. M.
A short history of Lakeland climbing/ by H. M. Kelly and J. H. Doughty.
See also DOUGHTY, J. H. (263)

KENNEDY, A. B. W. see MOORE, Adolphus Warburton (641)

KENNEDY, Edward Shirley see HUDSON, Charles (460)

496 KENNETT, John
The story of Annapurna/ retold and adapted by John Kennett from Maurice Herzog's "Annapurna. " - Bombay: Blackie & Son, 1955. - 72 p. : ill.

497 KESWICK MOUNTAIN RESCUE TEAM
Annual report. - Keswick; the Team, 1959.

498 KING, Clarence
Mountaineering in the Sierra Nevada, 1872/ by Clarence King. - London: Black, 1947. - 320 p. : 7 plates, bibl. , notes.
Entertaining personal notes of adventures of an early

American geologist. Includes climbing by lassoing outcrops, ice climbing with bowie knives and humorous
episodes. Ed.

499   KING, Thomas Starr
      The White Hills: their legends, landscape and po-
      etry/ by T. S. King. - Boston: 1862. - 403 p. : 60
      ill. , map.

500   KINGLEY, M. H.
      The ascent of Cameroons Peak and travels in French
      Congo/ by M. H. Kingsley. - Liverpool: 1896.

501   KINZL, Dr.
      Cordillera Huayhvash; 1954 Andes Recon/ by Doctor
      Kinzl.

502   KIRKPATRICK, William T.
      Alpine days and nights ... with a paper by the late
      R. Philip Hope, etc. / by William T. Kirkpatrick. -
      London: Alpine Club, 1932. - 198 p. : plates, port.
      Papers reprinted from the Alpine Journal.

503   KIRKUS, Colin F.
      Let's go climbing/ by Colin F. Kirkus. - London:
      Nelson, 1941 (1960 reprint). - 200 p. : 8 plates. (Nelson
      Juniors)
      "Introduction to climbing and fell walking mainly for
      boys and girls; illustrated with excellent accounts of
      climbs and shot through with enthusiasm. " NBL.

504   KLUCKER, Christian
      Adventures of an Alpine guide/ by Christian Klucker:
      trans. from the German by E. & P. von Gaisberg. Ed.
      with additional notes by H. E. G. Tyndale. - London:
      Murray, 1932.   329 p. : plates, ports.

505   KNOOP, Faith Yingling
      Sir Edmund Hillary/ by Faith Yingling Knoop; illus.
      by William Hutchinson. - London: F. Watts, 1974. -
      96 p. : col. ill. , maps, ports. , 22 cm. (Discovery books)
      Orig. pub. as A world explorer: Sir Edmund Hil-
      lary (Champaign, Ill. : Garrard, 1970).

506   KNOWLES, Archibald Campbell
      Adventures in the Alps/ by A. C. Knowles. - Lon-
      don: Skeffington & Son, 1913. - 175 p. : ill.

507 KNOWLTON, Elizabeth
    The naked mountains/ by Elizabeth Knowlton. -
New York: Putnam, 1933. - 335 p. : plates.
    Story of the German-American Himalayan Expedition
to Nanga Parbat. As the only woman on the expedition,
the author describes with penetration and understanding,
the attempt to climb the highest unclimbed, 7th highest
in the world, mountain--Nanga Parbat.

    KOGAN, Claude see LAMBERT, Raymond (514)

508 KOGAN, Georges
    The ascent of Alpamayo: an account of the Franco-
Belgian expedition to the Cordillera Blanca in the high
Andes/ by Georges Kogan and Nicole Leininger, trans.
from the French by Peter E. Thompson. - London:
Harrap, 1954. - 134 p. : plates.
    "6 French and 3 Belgians, including 2 wives attempt
to climb the Andes; they fail on Hauscaran, succeed on
Alpamayo and the wives establish a woman's record by
climbing Quitaraju alone. Charming tale. " BRD.

509 KOHLI, M. S.
    Last of the Annapurnas/ by M. S. Kohli. - Delhi:
Ministry of Information and Broadcasting, 1962. - 143
p. : 62 ill.
    "The account, told by the leader of the first ascent
of Annapurna III, by the Indian expedition in 1961. "
Yakushi.

510 _____.
    Nine atop Everest: story of the Indian ascent/ by
M. S. Kohli. - Bombay: Orient Longmans, 1969. -
384 p. : ill. , plates, 24 cm.
    "Story of the Indian ascent of Everest in 1965. "
Yakushi.

511 KOLB, Fritz
    Himalayan venture/ by Fritz Kolb; trans. from the
German by Lawrence Wilson. - London: Lutterworth,
1959. - 148 p. : 14 plates, maps, bibl. , 21 1/2 cm.
    Orig. pub. Munich, 1957.

511a KUGY, Julius
    Alpine pilgrimage/ by J. Kugy, trans. by H. E. G.
Tyndale. - London: Murray, 1934. - 374 p. : plates,
ports.

"Kugy was the Grand Old Man of the Julian Alps. He describes with gusto his days in these mountains in Yugoslavia followed by splendid Alpine seasons ... 1886-1913. " NBL.

512   .
      Son of the mountains: the life of an Alpine guide/ by Julius Kugy; trans. by H. E. G. Tyndale. - London: Nelson, 1838. - 198 p. : plates, port.

513   LAKE DISTRICT MOUNTAIN ACCIDENTS ASSOCIATION
      Report of advisory panel. - the Association, 1963.

514   LAMBERT, Raymond
      White fury: Gaurisanker and Cho Oyu/ by R. Lambert and Claude Kogan, trans. from the French by Showell Styles. - London: Hurst & Blackett, 1956. - 176 p. : 14 plates, maps, 21 cm.
      Orig. pub. Paris, 1955.
      See also DITTERT, Rene (260)

515   LANDOR, A. H. S.
      Everywhere: the memoirs of an explorer/ by A. H. S. Landor. - London: Unwin, 1924. - 596 p. : ill.
      "This contains the author's travels in Tibet of 1896-98. " Yakushi.

516   .
      Tibet and Nepal/ by A. H. S. Landor. - London: A. & C. Black, 1905. - 233 p. : 75 ill., map.
      "Highly imaginative account of the author's travels on the western border of Nepal in 1899. He crossed the Kali river at Garbyang, and explored in the region of Api-Nampa. And then he claimed he ascended the 23,490 peak, Nampa, and he travelled to Tinker. Finally he returned to Almora. " Yakushi.

517   LANE, Ferdinand Cole
      The story of mountains/ by Ferdinand C. Lane. - New York: Doubleday, 1950. - 488 p. : ill.

518   LANGDALE MOUNTAIN RESCUE TEAM
      Annual report. - Langdale: the Team, 1965.

519   LANGMUIR, Eric
      Mountain leadership: the official handbook of the Mountain Leadership Training Boards of Gt. Britain/ by

Eric Langmuir. - Edinburgh: Scottish Council of Physical Recreation, 1969.

520 LANGUEPIN, Jean-Jacques
To kiss high heaven: Nanda Devi: the epic story of eight young men on Nanda Devi/ by J. J. Languepin; trans. from the French by Mervyn Savill. - London: Kimber, 1956. - 199 p. : 6 plates, maps.
Orig. pub. Paris, 1955. "This is a tragic story of the Himalayan assaults. The French, led by Duplat, attempted in 1951 to climb Nanda Devi (first climbed in 1936), cross to mile-long ridge, and descend over East Nanda Devi. " Yakushi.

521 LARDEN, Walter
Argentine plains and Andine glaciers: life on an estancia, and an expedition into the Andes/ by Walter Larden. - London: Fisher Unwin, 1911. - 320 p. : 91 ill. , map.

522 _____.
Recollections of an old mountaineer/ by Walter Larden. - London: 1910. - 320 p. : 16 plates.

523 LATROBE, Charles J.
The Alpenstock/ by Charles J. Latrobe. - 2nd ed. - London: 1839.

LAWSON, Ralph see BENT, Allen Herbert (86)

524 LAYCOCK, John
Some shorter climbs in Derbyshire and elsewhere/ by John Laycock. - Manchester: Refuge Printing Dept. , 1913. - 116 p. : ill.

525 LE BLOND, Elizabeth Alice Frances
Adventures on the roof of the world/ by E. A. F. Le Blond. - London: Fisher Unwin, 1904. - xvi, 333 p. : ill.

526 _____.
Day in, day out: an autobiography/ by E. A. F. Le Blond. - London: John Lane, 1928. - 264 p. : 29 ill. port.

527 _____.
The high Alps in winter: or mountaineering in

search of health/ by Mrs. Fred Burnaby. - London:
Sampson Low & Co., 1883. - xvii, 204 p. : port.

528 .
_____ High life and towers of silence/ by E. A. F. Le
Blond. - London: Sampson Low & Co., 1886. - xii,
195 p. : plates.
"Proved that the high passes Tacul, Chardonnet,
Argentière and high peaks, such as the Aiguille du Midi
could be ascended in midwinter. " NBL.

529 .
_____ Mountaineering in the land of the Midnight Sun/ by
E. A. F. Le Blond. - London: Fisher Unwin, 1908. -
xii, 305 p. : 71 ill., map.

530 .
_____ True tales of mountain adventure for non-climbers
young and old/ by E. A. F. Le Blond. - London:
Fisher Unwin, 1903. - xvi, 199 p. : 35 plates, ports.

531 LECONTE, Joseph
A journal of ramblings through the high Sierra of
California by the University Excursion Party/ by Joseph
LeConte. - San Francisco: 1936. - 152 p. : ill., facsim.
of 1875 ed.

532 LE MESURIER, W. H.
An impromptu ascent of Mont Blanc/ by W. H. Le
Mesurier. - London: E. Stack, 1882. - 76 p.

533 LEONARD, Richard M.
Belaying the leader: an omnibus on climbing safety/
by Richard M. Leonard. - San Francisco: Sierra Club,
1956. - 85 p. : ill.
Highly technical and detailed manual of the theory of
climbing safety. The best evaluation of belaying yet
written. Ed.

534 LEPINEY, Jacques de
Climbs on Mont Blanc/ by Jacques and Tom de
Lepiney. - trans. by Sydney Spencer. - London: Edward
Arnold, 1930. - xii, 179 p. : plates.

535 .
_____ Climbs on Mt. McKinley/ by J. de Lepiney and T.
de Lepiney; trans. by Sydney Spencer. - London: Edward Arnold, 1930. - 179 p. : plates.

LEPINEY, Tom de see LEPINEY, Jacques de (534)

536 LEWIN, Walter Henry
    Climbs / by W. Lewin. - London: W. H. Smith &
Sons, 1932. - 226 p. : plates, ports.
    Also privately printed.

537 LEWIS, H. Warren
    You're standing on my fingers / by H. Warren
Lewis. - Berkeley, California: Howell-North Books,
1969. - 268 p. : ill. , maps, ports.

538 LIBRARY ASSOCIATION [Gt. Brit.] (Country Libraries
        Group)
    Mountaineering / 2nd ed. London: the Association,
1972. - 39 p. (Reader's guide no. 127)
    Approximately 350 titles of major mountaineering
interest with a brief note on many. A good introduction
to the general reader and novice mountaineer. Ed.

LISTER, George A. see CARR, Herbert Reginald Cul-
    ling (160)

LLOYD, F. H. see HOWARD, William D. (457)

539 LLOYD, Robert Wylie
    Dent Blanche, the E. Arete, reached from the
South / by Robert W. Lloyd. - London: 1913.

540 _____.
    The descent of the Brenva face of Mont Blanc / by
Robert W. Lloyd. - London: 1913.

541 _____.
    Episodes of two seasons / by Robert W. Lloyd. -
London: 1921.

542 _____.
    The first ascent of the French or north face of the
Col de Bionnassay / by Robert W. Lloyd. - London: 1920.

543 _____.
    Mont Blanc by the Brenva / by Robert W. Lloyd. -
London: 1913.

544 _____.
    A traverse of the Dent Blanche / by Robert W.
Lloyd. - London: 1927.

545 _____.
    Various expeditions in 1914/ by Robert W. Lloyd. - London: 1915.

546 LLOYD ALPINE COLLECTION
    Shelf catalogue of the Lloyd collection of Alpine books (in the National Library, Scotland)/ New York: Hall, 1965. - 94 p. : facsim. reprint of the orig. type- written and hand annotated copy.
    Lists approximately 2000 entries of multi-language works arranged in size order! 80% of entries were pre- 1900 and generally are difficult to use. Historical value only. Ed.

547 LONGLAND, Sir Jack
    Mountains and men/ by Sir Jack Longland. - Not- tingham: University Press, 1971. - 23 p. : plates, port. (Abbott memorial lectures, 1971)

548 LONGSTAFF, Thomas George
    Mountaineering/ by Tom Longstaff. - London: Lons- dale, n.d.

549 [no entry]

550 _____.
    This is my voyage: reminiscences of mountaineer- ing/ by Tom Longstaff. - London: Murray, 1950. - 324 p. : 23 plates, ill. , port. , maps.
    "A lifetime's journey in the Alps, Rockies, Arctic, Caucasus; but above all in the Himalaya. " NBL.

    LOVE, George see HILLARY, Sir Edmund Percival (433)

551 LOVELOCK, James
    Climbing/ by James Lovelock; with a chapter on artificial climbing by T. James. - London: Batsford, 1971. - 185 p. : 16 plates, ill.
    Appendix lists guides and mountain rescue posts and teams. An up-to-date book, and comprehensive it in- cludes history, equipment, and techniques. Worth hav- ing to update the majority of mountaineering books. Ed.

552 LOWE, George
    Because it is there/ George Lowe. - London: Cas- sell, 1959. - 224 p. : ill. , maps.

553 _____.
From Everest to the South Pole/ by George Lowe. -
New York: St. Martin's Press, 1961. - 216 p. : ill. ,
maps.
"The author climbed high on Everest in 1953 and
crossed the Antarctic in 1957-58. This book includes
the New Zealand Garhwal expedition of 1951, the Cho
Oyu expedition of 1952, and the New Zealand Barun expedition of 1954. " Yakushi.

554 LOWERY, L. G.
Mountains are for climbing/ by L. G. Lowery. -
San Antonio: Naylor, 1973.

555 LUKAN, Karl
Alps and alpinism/ ed. by K. Lukan; trans. from
the German by Hugh Merrick, intro. by Chris Boning-
ton. - 200 p. : ill. , facsims. , ports.
A well-illustrated history; includes photographs.
See also NOYCE, Wilfred Cuthbert Francis (705)

556 _____.
Mountain adventures/ by Karl Lukan. - London:
Collins, 1972. - 128 p. : col. ill. , ports. , bibl. (Inter-
national library)

557 LUNN, Sir Arnold Henry Moore
Alpine skiing at all heights and seasons/ 3rd ed. -
London: Methuen, 1948. - 106 p. 8.
First pub. 1921.

558 _____.
The Bernese Oberland/ by Sir Arnold Lunn. - London: Eyre and Spottiswoode, 1958. - 215 p. : front. ,
16 plates.

559 _____.
A century of mountaineering/ by Sir Arnold Lunn. -
London: Allen & Unwin, 1955. - 263 p. : 23 plates.

560 _____.
The Englishman in the Alps/ ed. by Sir Arnold
Lunn. - London: Oxford University Press, 1913. -
294 p.
"An admirable collection of English prose and poetry
relating to the Alps: John Evelyn to Geoffrey Winthrop
Young. " NBL.

561 .

    Matterhorn centenary/ by Sir Arnold Lunn. - London: Allen & Unwin, 1965. - 144 p. : 24 plates.

A history of the Matterhorn written by a member of the pre-piton school of mountaineering; recreates vividly the spirit of the age. Ed.

562 .

    Memory to memory/ by Sir Arnold Lunn. - London: Hollis & Carter, 1956. - 268 p. : front. (port.), plates, Autobiography.

563 .

    Mountain jubilee/ by Sir Arnold Lunn. - London: Eyre and Spottiswoode, 1943. - 287 p. : plates.

564 .

    Mountains of memory/ by Sir Arnold Lunn. - London: Macmillan, 1949. - 248 p. : plates.

"Memoirs of fifty years skiing and mountaineering. A collection of people, places, and thoughts against the background of the mountains. " BRD.

565 .

    Mountains of youth/ by Sir Arnold Lunn. London: Milford, 1925; Eyre & Spottiswoode, 1949.

"The first English ski-mountaineering book. Mr. Lunn is a capable summer climber, ... [but is famous for] his pioneer ski-climbs and ski-tours across the Oberland, Monte Rosa and Eiger from 1908. " BRD.

566 .

    Oxford mountaineering essays/ by Sir Arnold Lunn. - London: Edward Arnold, 1912. - 237 p.

567 .

    The Swiss and their mountains: a study of the influence of mountains on men/ by Sir Arnold Lunn. - London: Allen & Unwin, 1963. - 168 p. : 23 plates, 21 1/2 cm.

Dealing with the early history of the Alps, the author describes Rousseau and the mountain cult, early mountaineers Alpine guides, and the effect of tourism on the Swiss. Ed.

568 .

    Switzerland: Her topographical, historical and literary landmarks/ by Sir Arnold Lunn. - London: Harrap, 1928. - 320 p. : ill. , plates. (Kitbag travel books)

569 _____.
Switzerland and the English/ by Sir Arnold Lunn. - London: Eyre & Spottiswoode, 1944. - x, 258 p. : plates.

570 _____.
Switzerland in English prose and poetry/ by Sir Arnold Lunn. - London: Eyre and Spottiswoode, 1947. - ill.
A selection from the works of English writers on Switzerland; mostly on climbing in the Alps. Ed.

571 _____.
Unskilled for so long/ by Sir Arnold Lunn. - London: Allen & Unwin, 1968. - 175 p. : plates, port.

572 _____.
Zermatt and the Valois/ by Sir Arnold Lunn. - London: Hallis & Carter, 1955. - 211 p. : plates.

572a LYTH, John C.
First aid in mountain rescue/ by John C. Lyth. - n. p. : privately printed, 1961. - 24 p.

573 McCALLUM, John D.
Everest diary/ by John D. McCallum, foreword by James Ramsey Ullman. - Chicago: Follett, 1966. - 213 p. : ill.
Based on the personal diary of Lute Jersted, one of the first five Americans to conquer Mt. Everest. Ed.

574 MacDONALD, Hugh, ed.
On foot: an anthology/ ed. by Hugh MacDonald. - Oxford: U. P. , 1942. - 320 p.

575 MacGREGOR, John
The ascent of Mont Blanc/ by John MacGregor. - (S. L.): 1853.

576 MacINNES, Hamish
Climbing/ by Hamish MacInnes. - Stirling: Scottish Y. H. A. , 1964.

577 _____.
International mountain rescue handbook/ ed. by

Hamish MacInnes. - London: Constable, 1972. - 218
p. : illus. , bibl.
An up-to-date handbook of equipment, technique and
practice of interest to all rock climbers, mountaineers
and skiers. Large section on avalanches; well illustrated. Ed.

578
_____ Scottish climbs: a mountaineer's pictorial guide to
climbing in Scotland/ by Hamish MacInnes. - London:
Constable, 1971. 2 vols.

578a MacINTOSH, A. J.
Mountaineering clubs: 1857-1907/ A. J. MacIn-
tosh. - London: Eyre & Spottisoode, 1908. - 31 p.
See also COCKBURN, Henry (199)

579 MacINTYRE, Donald
Hindu-Koh: wanderings and wild sport on and beyond the high Himalayas/ by Donald MacIntyre. - New
ed. - London: Blackwood, 1891. - 362 p. : illus.

580 MacINTYRE, Neil
Attack on Everest/ by Neil MacIntyre. - London:
Methuen, 1936. - 171 p. : illus.
"Chapters 1-8 give a history of Everest itself, from
its discovery till the 5th expedition of 1936. Chapt. 9,
the first ascent of Kamet of 1931 by Smythe; and Chapt.
10, Kangchenjunga expeditions in 1929 and 1931 under
P. Bauer, and in 1930 under G. O. Dyrenfurth. But
the author knows nothing of mountains or of the Himalaya. " Yakushi.

McLAREN, F. D. see FIELD, Ernest K. (317)

McMORRIN, Ian see NOYCE, Wilfred (713)

581 McMORRIS, William Bruce
The real book of mountaineering/ by W. B. Mc-
Morris; illus. by Albert Orbaan. - London: Dobson,
1961. - 192 p. : illus. , bibl. (Real books; ed. by Patrick Pringle)

582 MAEDER, Herbert
The mountains of Switzerland: the adventure of the
high Alps/ ed. with photographs and commentary by H.
Maeder; with an introd. by Werner Kampfen and contrib.
by Georges Grosjean and Ricco Bianchi. Trans. from

the German by Hendrik P. B. Betlem. - London: Allen
& Unwin, 1968. - 288 p. : (16 fold), ill. , facsim. , maps.
Orig. pub. as Die Berge der Schweiz. Olten: Wal-
ter Verlag, 1967.

583 MAGNONE, Guido
The west face/ by G. Magnone, trans. from the
French by J. F. Burke. - London: Museum Press,
1955. - 166 p. , plates.
The first ascent of the "Petit Dru". Ed.

584 MAGUIRE, T. Miller
Strategy and tactics in mountain ranges/ by T. Miller Maguire. - London: William Clewes & Sons, 1904. -
172 p. : maps, 25 cm.

MAIN, Mrs. E. see Le BLOND, Elizabeth Alice Frances

585 MAITLAND, Frederic William
Life and letters of Leslie Stephen/ by F. W. Maitland. - London: Duckworth, 1906. - viii, 510 p.

586 MALARTIC, Yves
Tenzing of Everest/ by Yves Malartic, trans. from
the French by Judith B. Heller. - New York: Crown
Publishers, 1954. - 285 p. : ill.
"A controversial biography disclaimed by Tenzing;
it reflects a bias toward the Sherpas at the expense of
the British. Can not be classed as an official account. "
BRD.

587 MALLIK, B. N.
The sky was his limit: the life and climbs of Sonam
Gyatso/ by B. N. Mallik. - Dehra Dun: Palit & Dutt,
1970. - 200 p. : plates, 21 cm.

MALLORY, George Leigh see PYE, David (776); RO-
BERTSON, David (807); STYLES, Frank Showell (944)

587a MANDOLF, Henry I.
Basic mountaineering/ ed. by H. I. Mandolf. - San
Diego, Calif. : Sierra Club, 1961. - 112 p. : ill.
Excellent for beginners--equipment, first aid, snow
climbing, desert travel and alpine rescue. Ed.

588 MANNERING, George Edward
With axe and rope in the New Zealand Alps/ by G.

E. Mannering. - London: Longmans, 1891. - 139 p. : ill.

589 _____.
      The Franz Josef glacier, New Zealand / by G. E.
Mannering. - Christchurch, N. Z. : Whitcombe & Tombs,
1930. - plates with letterpress.

590 _____.
      Mount Cook and its surrounding glaciers / by G. E.
Mannering. - Auckland: Whitcomb & Tombs, 1930.
Folio of photographs with text. Ed.

MANNING, Harvey see THE MOUNTAINEERS, Seattle
     (666) & MILLER, Thomas Wayne (617)

591 MARIANI, Fosco
     Karakorum: the ascent of Gasherbrum IV / by Fos-
co Maraiani; trans. from the Italian by James Cadell. -
London: Hutchinson, 1961. - 320 p. : 80 plates, tables,
23 cm.
     Orig. pub. 1959. This book is very much concern-
ed with the inhabitants, religions, origins and history of
this fantastically majestic mountain range. The author
vividly describes his personal involvement on this expedition. Ed.

591a _____.
     Where four worlds meet: Hindu Kush, 1959 / by
Fosco Mariani, trans. from the Italian by Peter Green;
maps by Joan Emerson. - London: Hamish Hamilton,
1964. - 290 p. : 100 plates, maps, 23 1/2 cm.
     "Account of a successful Italian ascent of Saraghrar
in North Chitral in 1959. " Yakushi.

592 MARINER, Wastl
     Mountain rescue techniques / by W. Mariner; rev.
by Otto T. Trott. - Innsbruck: Austrian Alpine Association, in association with the Mountaineers, 1963. -
200 p. : ill. , bibl.
     First pub. 1948. Though dated in parts, it is still
very relevant to rescue methods. Contains interest on
equipment and normal mountaineering techniques. Ed.

593 MARSH, Herbert Elliott
     Two seasons in Switzerland / by Herbert Elliott
Marsh. - London: Unwin, 1895. - ill.

593a MARSHALL, Howard Percival
Men against Everest/ by Howard Marshall. - London: Country Life, 1954. - 64 p. : plates, 2 maps.
"Short history of Mount Everest up to the first ascent. " Yakushi.

MARTEL, Pierre see WINDHAM, William (1104)

MASON, B. R. see FEDERATED MOUNTAIN CLUBS OF NEW ZEALAND (312)

594 MASON, Gene W.
Minus three/ by G. W. Mason. - Englewood Cliffs, N. J. , Prentice-Hall, 1970. - 190 p. : ill.

595 MASON, Kenneth
The abode of snow: a history of Himalayan exploration and mountaineering/ by Kenneth Mason. - London: Hart Davis, 1955. - 372 p. : 19 plates, maps, bibl.
"First authoritative history of Himalayan exploration. " NBL.

596 _____ .
Routes in the Western Himalaya, Kashmir etc. / by K. Mason. - Government of India Press, 1929.

MASSACHUSETTS INSTITUTE OF TECHNOLOGY OUTING CLUB see M. I. T. OUTING CLUB (626)

597 MATTHEWS, Charles Edward
The annals of Mt. Blanc: a monograph ... / by C. E. Mathews; with a chapter on the geology of the mountain by Prof. T. G. Bonney. - London: Fisher Unwin, 1898. - 368 p. : bibl.
"A history, by one of the founders of the Alpine Club, of the mountain from the days of de Saussure to the building of an observatory (since disappeared). " NBL.

598 MATHEWS, Charles Edward
An ascent of the Matterhorn from the south side/ by C. E. Mathews. - London: 1871.

599 _____ .
Mountaineering/ by C. E. Mathews. - London: Dent, 1892.
See also GEORGE, Hereford Brooke (358)

600 MAYDON, D. C.
    Simen: its heights and abysses; a record of travel
and sport in Abyssinia with some account of the sacred
city / by H. C. Maydon. - London: Witherby, 1925. -
244 p. : ill. , maps.

601 MAZAMA: A record of mountaineering in the Pacific
Northwest
    Pub. by the Mazamas, vol. 1, 1890.

602 MAZEAUD, Pierre
    Naked before the mountain / by Pierre Mazeud; with
a preface by Walter Bonatti; trans. from the French by
Geoffrey Sutton. - London: Gollancz, 1974. - 256 p. :
24 p. , ill. , ports. , 23 cm.
    Orig. pub. in German trans. : Schritte himmelwarts;
Heering, 1968; and in French: Montagne pour une homme.
nu; Arthaud, 1971.

603 MAZUCHELI, Nina Elizabeth
    The Indian Alps and how we crossed them: being a
narrative of two years residence in the Eastern Himalaya and two months tour into the interior / by a lady
pioneer. - London: 1876.

604 MEADE, Charles Francis
    Approach to the hills / by C. F. Meade. - London:
Murray, 1940. - 265 p. : plates.
    'Narratives of some notorious modern climbs--North
face of the Matterhorn, Grand Jorasses, Eigerwand--to-
gether with some of the author's own climbs. " NBL.

605
    High mountains / by C. F. Meade. - London: Har-
vill, 1954. - 136 p. : plates.

606 MEANY, Edmond Stephen
    Mount Rainier: a record of exploration / ed. by
E. S. Meany. - New York: Macmillan, 1916. - 325 p. :
ill.

607 MELBOURNE UNIVERSITY MOUNTAINEERING CLUB
    Equipment for mountaineering: a guide to the choice
of equipment for the bush walker, rock climber, caver,
and mountaineer. - 2nd ed. - Melbourne University
Press, 1965. - 120 p.

608 MELDRUM, Kim
Artificial climbing walls/ by K. Meldrum and B.
Royle. - London: Pelham, 1970. - 69 p.: 12 plates, ill.

MENDENHALL, John see MENDENHALL, Ruth (609)

609 MENDENHALL, Ruth
Introduction to rock and mountain climbing/ by Ruth
and John Mendenhall; illus. by Vivian Mendenhall; -
Harrisburg, Pa.: Stackpole Books, 1969. - 192 p.: ill.

MERRICK, Hugh, pseud. see MEYER, Harold Albert

610 MERZBACHER, Gottfried
The Central Tian-shan mountains: 1902-1903, etc./
by G. Merzbacher. - London: Royal Geographical Society of London, 1905. - 294 p.: ill., maps.

611 MEYER, Hans Heinrich Joseph
Across East African glaciers: an account of the
first ascent of Kilamanjaro/ by H. H. J. Meyer; trans.
from the German by E. H. S. Calder, London: Philip
& Sons, 1891. - 404 p.: ill., maps, bibl., appendices.

612 _____.
In the high Andes of Ecuador: Chimborazo, Cotopaxi, etc. ... portfolio of plates. 24 large quarto
chrome-lithographic plates from paintings by Rudolf Res-
chreiter and 20 plates with 40 phototypes from the ori-
ginals of various artists and explorers/ by H. H. J.
Meyer, with a preface and 24 pages of explanatory text. -
London: Williams and Norgate, 1908.

613 _____.
Rambles in the Alps/ by H. H. J. Meyer. - Trans-
atlantic, 1952.

614 MEYER, Harold Albert
The perpetual hills: a personal anthology of moun-
tains/ comp. by Hugh Merrick (pseud.). London:
Newnes, 1964. - 247 p.: 32 plates.
Combining an autobiographical account of the author's
experiences with an anthology of prose and poetry on the
subject, the book has much enthusiasm for an interested
reader. Ed.

615 _____.
Savoy episodes/ by Hugh Merrick (pseud.). - London:

Robert Hale, 1946. - 192 p. : plates.
Mountaineering holidays in the French Alps. Ed.

616 MICHELET, Jules
The mountain / by Jules Michelet, trans. from the
French by the translator of "The Bird" (W. H. D.
Adams) with ill. from designs by P. Skelton. - Edin-
burgh: 1872. - 323 p. : 54 ill.
"Chapters on the Alps, Mont Blanc, the Pyrenees,
Java, alpine flowers and plants, etc. " Dawson's.

MILLAR, J. Halket see ALACK, Frank (16)

617 MILLER, Thomas Wayne
Photographs by Tom Miller: the North Cascades /
text by Harvey Manning; maps and sketches by Dee Molenaar. - Seattle: The Mountaineers, 1964 - 95 p. ;
ill. , maps.

618 MILLS, Emos Abijah
Adventures of a nature guide / by E. A. Mills. -
New York: Doubleday, 1920.
A narrative by an outdoorsman and his personal ex-
periences which include mountain climbing. Recommend-
ed for boy scouts. Ed.

619 MILLS, James
Airborne to the mountains / by James Mills. - Lon-
don: Jenkins, 1961. - 202 p. : plates, ports. , map,
table.
The British Army Parachute Brigade expedition to
Alaska, 1956. Ed.

620 MILNE, Lorus Johnson
The mountains / by L. J. and Margery J. G. Milne
and the editors of "Life". - New York: Time, 1962. -
192 p. : ill. , 28 cm. (Life nature library)

621 MILNE, Malcolm
The book of modern mountaineering / ed. by M.
Milne, with a foreword by Lord Hunt of Llanvair Water-
dine. - New York: Putnam, 1968. - 304 p. : ill. , ports.
Essays and photographs by experts: up to date in
dealing with "free" and "artificial" climbing and gener-
ous in its world coverage. Ed.

MILNE, Margery J. G. see MILNE, Lorus Johnson
(620)

622 MILNER, Cyril Douglas
     The Dolomites / by C. D. Milner. - London: Hale,
1951. - 105 p. : 150 ill. , 7 maps, plates.

623 _____.
     Mont Blanc and the Aiguilles / by C. D. Milner. -
London: Hale, 1955. - 176 p. : 70 ill. , 64 plates, maps,
bibl.

624 _____.
     Mountain photography: its art and technique in Bri-
tain and abroad / by C. D. Milner. - London: Focal
Press, 1945. - 238 p.

625 _____.
     Rock for climbing / illus. with 97 photographs by
the author. - London: Chapman and Hall, 1950. - 128
p. : front. , ill.

626 M. I. T. OUTING CLUB
     Fundamentals of climbing / by the M. I. T. Outing
Club. - 46 p.

627 MITCHELL, Dick
     Mountaineering first aid: a guide to accident res-
ponse and first aid / by Dick Mitchell. - 96 p. : 24 ill.
     "Compact, concise handbook. Covers immediate
care for wounds, shock, fractures, common emergencies
and high altitude problems; plus preparation for rescue. "
Speleobooks.

628 MITCHELL, Elyne
     Australia's alps / by E. Mitchell. - New Ed. - Lon-
don: Angus & Robertson, 1963. - 185 p. : 16 plates,
maps. First pub. 1942

629 [no entry]

630 MOFFAT, Gwen
     On my home ground / by Gwen Moffat. - London:
Hodder and Stoughton, 1968. - 256 p. : ill. , 15 plates.
     An autobiographical story of making a home in rural
remoteness; encompassing the roles of housewife, mountaineer, guide, rescuer and author. Ed.

631 _____.
     Space below my feet / by Gwen Moffat. - London:

Hodder and Stoughton, 1961. - 286 p. : 6 plates.

632 _____.
Survival count: autobiography/ by Gwen Moffat. -
London: Gollancz, 1972. - 175 p. : ill., maps, bibl.
Concerned mainly with the conservation of the moun-
tains and other wildernesses. Ed.

633 _____.
Two star red: a book about R. A. F. mountain
rescue/ by Gwen Moffat. - London: Hodder & Stoughton, 1964. - 206 p. : maps, 6 plates.
This history of British Mountain Rescue, which includes nine years personal experience provides a general introduction. Ed.

634 MOLENAAR, Dee
The challenge of Rainier: a record of the explorations and ascents, triumphs and tragedies, on the northwest's greatest mountain/ by D. Molenaar. - Seattle:
The Mountaineers, 1971. - 332 p. : ill.

635 MOLONY, Eileen
Portraits of mountains/ by E. Molony. - London:
Dobson, 1950. - 118 p. : 11 plates.
Eleven essays on British mountains: eight of them
originated as broadcasts for the Third Programme. Ed.

636 MONKHOUSE, Frank
Climber and fellwalker in Lakeland/ by F. Monkhouse and Joe Williams. - Newton Abbot: David Charles, 1972. - 214 p. : ill., maps, bibl.

637 MONTAGNIER, Henry F.
A bibliography of the ascents of Mont Blanc from
1761 1853/ by H. F. Montagnier; reprinted from the
Alpine Journal, August 1911. - London: Spottiswoode &
Co., 1911. - 35 p.

638 _____.
A further contribution to the bibliography of Mont
Blanc, 1786-1853/ by H. F. Montagnier. - London: 1916.

639 _____.
Pamphlets on the Alps/ by H. F. Montagnier

640 MOON, Kenneth William
Man of Everest: the story of Sir Edmund Hillary/

by Kenneth W. Moon. - London: Lutterworth Press, 1962. - 96 p. : bibl. (Courage and conquest series, no. 7)

641   MOORE, Adolphus Warburton
The Alps in 1864: a private journal/ ed. by A. B. W. Kennedy. - Edinburgh: David Douglas, 1902. - 444 p. : ill. , 2nd ed. / by E. H. Stevens. Oxford, Blackwell, 1939.   2vols. (Blackwell's mountaineering library)
Account of an Alpine season, in the company of Whymper, with an ascent of Mt. Blanc from the Brenva glacier. Ed.
See also EBERLI, Henry (283)

642   MOORE, Terris
Mt. McKinley: the pioneer climbs/ by Terris Moore. - University of Alaska Press, 1967. - 202 p. : ill. , maps.

643   MORDECAI, D.
The Himalayas: an illustrated summary of the world's highest mountain ranges/ by D. Mordecai. - Chesterfield, Derbyshire: R. Redford, 1969. - 28 p. : 30 ill.

644   MORDEN, William J.
Across Asia's snows and deserts/ by William J. Morden, introduction by Roy Chapman Andrews. - New York: 1927. - 414 p. : 65 ill.
"From Kashmir, across the Himalaya and Karakoram ranges, into the Russian Pamirs and northwest to Thian Shan; then to Mongolia and Siberia. " Dawson's.

645   MORIN, Micheline
Everest: from the first attempt to the final victory/ by Micheline Morin. - London: Harrap, 1955. - 205 p. : ill. , plates, 20 cm.
An account of ten attempts since 1922 to the final assault in 1953.   Written for high school students and older, with a subsidiary interest in flora and fauna on the approach marches. Ed.

646   MORIN, Nea
A woman's reach: mountaineering memoirs/ by Nea Morin. - London: Eyre & Spottiswoode, 1968. - 288 p. : ill. , 25 plates, maps.
Memoir of one of Britain's best known woman moun-

taineers, who has climbed with Eric Shipton and Christian Bonington among others.   Includes a list of the first
feminine ascents. Ed.

647   MORRIS, J.
      Hired to kill: some chapters of autobiography/ by
J. Morris. - London: Hart-Davis, 1960. - 272 p. : map.
      "His chapters on Mount Everest make excellent
reading and some chapters include an account of his
journey with H. F. Montagnier in 1927 in Hunza Area,
north of Distaghil Sar up to the Mintaka Pass and the
Tagdumbash Pamir. " Yakushi.

648   _____ .
      A winter in Nepal/ by J. Morris. - London: Hart-
Davis, 1963. - 232 p. : 46 ill. , map.
      "This book, by a member of the 1922 and 1936
Mount Everest expeditions, gives a life in the villages
of Nepal. " Yakushi.

649   MORRIS, James Humphrey
      Coronation Everest/ by James Morris. - London:
Faber, 1958. - 146 p. : 7 plates, 3 maps.
      "The author was the special correspondent of The
Times.   This book is the story of how the news of the
ascent of Everest reached London in 1953. " Yakushi.

650   MOSSO, Angelo
      Life of man on the high Alps/ by Angelo Mosso. -
London: Fisher Unwin, 1898. - 342 p. : ill.

651   MOULD, Daphne Desiree Charlotte Pochin
      Mountains of Ireland/ by D. Mould. - London: Bats-
ford, 1955. - 160 p. : front, 47 ill. , map, bibl.

652   MOUNT EVEREST COMMITTEE
      Catalogue of the exhibition of photographs and paint-
ings from the Mount Everest Expedition, 1922. - n. p. :
the Committee, 1923. - 9 p. : ill.

653   THE MOUNT EVEREST EXPEDITIONS OF 1921 AND 1922
      Three lectures; with description of lantern slides. -
London, Newton, 1925. - 60 p.

654   [no entry]

655   MOUNTAIN CLUB OF KENYA
      Mountain Rescue Unit instructions. - Nairobi: The

Mountain Club of Kenya, 1963.

656 THE MOUNTAIN CODE (Compiled by members of a
Working Party at the suggestion of the British Mountaineering Council).
London: Central Council of Physical Education,
1968. - 16 p. : ill. , 19 cm. Chairman: Lord Hunt.

657 MOUNTAIN RESCUE COMMITTEE
Accident reports. - Manchester: The Committee,
1961.

658 _____.
Mountain rescue and cave rescue. - New ed. -
Manchester: The Committee, 1970. - 72 p. : ill. , maps.

659 MOUNTAIN WORLD
The mountain world/ by the Swiss Foundation for
Alpine Research. - London: Allen & Unwin, 1953-70. -
10 v.
Orig. title: Berge der Welt. Publication ceased in
1970 with the 10th vol. (1968-69). Several English editions were ed. by Malcolm Barnes. Ed.

660 THE MOUNTAINEER, Big Sandy, Montana
History of Big Sandy, Montana. - Montana: Big
Sandy, 1957. - 37 p. : ill.

661 MOUNTAINEERING ASSOCIATION
Elementary mountaineering. - The Mountaineering
Association, 1951.

662 _____.
Mountain holidays: graded courses in mountaineer-
ing at the finest climbing centres in Britain and the
Alps. - London: The Association, 1967. - 25 p. : ill.

663 MOUNTAINEERING IN CHINA
Peking: 1965. - mostly illustrations.

664 THE MOUNTAINEERS, SEATTLE.
The mountaineer climber's notebook. - Seattle: The
Mountaineers, 1946. - 135 p. : ill.

665 _____.
Mountaineering: the freedom of the hills, planned
by the climbing Committee of the Mountaineers/ Harvey

Manning, Chairman of editors. - Seattle: The Mountaineers, 1960. - 430 p. : ill.

666
———.
Mountaineer's handbook: the techniques of mountain
climbing/ by the Mountaineers, Inc. for the Mountaineering Club of Seattle. - Seattle: Superior Pub. , 1948. -
160 p. : ill.
A comprehensive little book designed to fit into a
rucksack.

667 MUIR, John
The mountains of California/ by John Muir. New York:
1894. - 381p.
Spontaneous emotion over everyting in the Sierras. Ed.

668
———.
The Yosemite/ by John Muir. - "A flow of enthusiasm and inspiration. " Ed.

669 MULGREW, Peter
I hold the heights/ by Peter Mulgrew. - New York:
Doubleday, 1965. - 204 p. : ill.
'Including the Makalu expedition in 1960-61 under
E, Hillary. " Yakushi. Probably the American ed. of
No place for men (670). Ed.

670
———.
No place for men/ by Peter Mulgrew. - London;
Vane, 1965. - 199 p. : 24 plates.
The account of Sir Edmund Hillary's 1900 expedition
to research the physiological effects of high altitude
climbing without oxygen. A well written account of how
the author collapsed with pulmonary thrombosis 350 feet
below the summit of Makalu and his loss of several
fingers and both legs. Ed

671 MULLER, Edwin
They climbed the Alps/ by Edwin Muller. - London:
Jonathan Cape: 1930. - 215 p. : plates.
Although none of the material is new, the author has
selected extracts from famous narratives connected by a
commentary. A good examination in style and presenta-
tion of mountaineering literature. Ed.

672 MUMM, Arnold Louis
The Alpine Club Register, 1857-1863, 1864-1876,

1877-1890, 1923-1928/ by Arnold Louis Mumm. - London: The Alpine Club.

673 _____ .

Five months in the Himalaya: a record of mountain travel in Garhwal and Kashmir/ by Arnold Louis Mumm. London: Edward Arnold, 1909. - 263 p. : ill. , maps.

"Account of the author's mountaineering expedition with Bruce and Longstaff to the ranges in Garhwal and afterwards with Bruce to Kashmir in 1907. At that time, Longstaff with two Italian guides successfully ascended Trisul. " Yakushi.

674 MUMMERY, Alfred Frederick
Further explorations in the Caucasus/ by A. F. Mummery and others. - London: 1889.

675 _____ .

My climbs in the Alps and Caucasus/ by Alfred Frederick Mummery. - London: Cassell, 1895. - 360 p. : ill.

Reflects the change of emphasis in climbing--the making of new, difficult routes up classic peaks rather than new ascents--and the new interest in rock climbing for its own sake. Ed.

See also UNSWORTH, Walter (1035)

MUNCHAUSEN, Baron see GEORGE, Hereford Brooke (358)

676 MUNDAY, Walter Alfred Don
Mt. Garibaldi Park: Vancouver's alpine playground/ by W. A. D. Munday. - Vancouver: 1922. - 47 p.

677 _____ .

The unknown mountain: Mt. Waddington, British Columbia/ by W. A. D. Munday. - London: Hodder & Stoughton, 1948. - 268 p. : plates, map.

Tough pioneering in British Columbia where the hazards of approach to the mountains include whirlpools, virgin forest and grizzlies. Ed.

678 MUNDELL, Frank
Stories of alpine adventure/ by F. Mundell. - London: Sunday School Union, 1898. - 158 p.

679 MUNRO, Sir Hugh Thomas
Munro's tables of the 3,000 foot mountains of Scot-

land and other tables of lesser heights. - 1954 rev. ed/
by J. C. Donaldson and W. L. Coats. - Goring: West
Col. , 1969. - 69 p. : ill. , index.

680   MURRAY, John
        Murray's Handbook for Switzerland, the Alps of Sa-
      voy and Piedmont, including the Protestant valleys of
      the Waldenses/ London: Murray, 1838. - lix, 367 p. :
      ill. , map.

680a   .
        Murray's Knapsack guide to the Tyrol and the East-
      ern Alps/ London: Murray, 1867.
        Murray published numerous guides to England, Eu-
      ope and elsewhere; most were of interest to travelers
      and not climbers. Ed.

681   MURRAY, William Hutchison
        The craft of climbing/ by W. H. Murray and J. E.
      B. Wright. - London: Kaye and Ward, 1964. - 77 p. :
      16 plates, tables, 21 1/2 cm.
        Expert advice on rock, ice and snow climbing, with
      lessons drawn from the greatest climbs of all. Ed.

682   .
        Mountaineering in Scotland/ by W. H. Murray. -
      London: Dent, 1947. - 252 p. : 15 plates, maps, diags.

683   .
        Scottish Himalayan expedition/ by W. H. Murray. -
      London: Dent, 1955.
        Climbing and exploration in Kumaon. Ed.

684   .
        The story of Everest/ by W. H. Murray; illus. by
      Robert Anderson. - London: Dent, 1953. - 193 p. : ill.
        A popular history of all attempts on the mountain
      up to success in 1953. Ed.

685   .
        Undiscovered Scotland: climbs on rock, snow and
      ice/ by W. H. Murray; with 14 maps and diagrams by
      Robert Anderson. - London: Dent, 1951. - 232 p. :
      plates, ill. , maps.
        Accounts of a number of remarkable winter climbs
      in 1937 and 1938, which illustrate the ever rising stan-
      dard of achievement on British hills. Ed.

NAESS, Arne see NORWEGIAN HIMALAYAN EXPEDITION (701)

686 NASH, T. A.
A day and a night on the Aiguille du Dru/ by T. A. Nash. - London: 1889.

NATIONAL SKI ASSOCIATION OF AMERICA see BROWER, David Ross (123)

687 NAVARRA, Fernand
The forbidden mountain/ by Fernand Navarra; trans. from the French by Michael Legat. - London: MacDonald, 1956. - 176 p. : 14 plates, 2 maps.
Orig. pub. as L'Expedition au Mont Ararat; Bordeaux, 1953.

NEILL, John see JONES, Trevor (493)

688 NESBIT, Paul W.
Longs peak: its story and a guide for climbing it/ by Paul W. Nesbit. - Colorado Springs: Out West Printing and Stationery Co. , 1946. - 47 p. : ill.

689 NEVE, Arthur
Thirty years in Kashmir/ by Arthur Neve. - London: Edward Arnold, 1913. - 316 p. : ill. , map.
Dr. Neve was in charge of the Kashmir Mission Hospital at Strinagur, but devoted his spare time to mountaineering expeditions on Nanga Parbat, Nun Kun and other giants of the Himalayas. Ed.

690 NEVE, Ernest Frederic
Beyond the Pir Panjal: life among the mountains and valleys of Kashmir/ by E. F. Neve. - London: Fisher Unwin, 1912. - 320 p.
Popular ed. pub. London: Church Missionary Society, 1914. - 178 p.

691 NEW, Charles
Life, wanderings and labours in Eastern Africa with an account of the first successful ascent of the equatorial snow mountain, Kilimanjaro and remarks on the East African slavery/ by Charles New. - London: Hodder and Stoughton, 1873. - 525 p. : ill. , maps.

692 THE NEW ASCENT OF MONT BLANC
London: 1854.

693 NEW ZEALAND ALPINE CLUB
Rules/ (S. L.): The Club, 1933.

694 NEWBY, Eric
A short walk in the Hindu Kush/ by Eric Newby. -
London: Secker & Warburg, 1958. - 247 p.: 8 plates,
2 maps.
"The story of the novices travelling in the country,
and trying to climb a peak of 19,800 ft. In the Afghan
Hindu Kush. " Yakushi.

695 NICHOLSON, Norman
The lakers: the adventures of the first tourists,
etc. / by Norman Nicholson. - London: Robert Hale,
1955. - 235 p.: plates.

NIMLIN, J. B.   see WILSON, John Douglas Bruce (1103)

696 NOCK, Peter
Rock climbing/ by Peter Nock. - London: Foyle,
1963. - 95 p.: 10 plates, 11 ill.

697 NOEL, John Baptist Lucius
The story of Everest, etc. / by J. B. L. Noel.
Boston: Little, Brown, 1927. - 258 p.: plates.
By the official photographer of the 1922 and 1929
Mount Everest expeditions. He describes Mallory and
Irvine's climb to within 600 feet of the summit, when
they were seen before disappearing. Ed.

698 _____.
Through Tibet to Everest/ by J. B. L. Noel. -
London: Edward Arnold, 1927. - 302 p.: plates, ports.
An account of the 1924 expedition on which the au-
thor was a photographer. Ed.

699 NORMAN-NERUDA, May
The Climbs of [Louis] Norman-Neruda/ ed. by M.
Norman-Neruda, and with an account of his last climb. -
London: Fisher Unwin, 1899. - 335 p.: ill.

700 NORTON, Edward Felix
The fight for Everest/ by Lt. Col. E. F. Norton
and with other members of the expedition. - London:
Arnold, 1924. - 372 p.: maps, ill., plates.
Remarkable photography, vivid and thrilling narra-
tive; definitely recommended. Ed.

701 NORWEGIAN HIMALAYAN EXPEDITION (1949)
      Tirich Mir / by members of the Norwegian Hima-
laya expedition; trans. by Salvi and Richard Bateson. -
London: Hodder and Stoughton, 1952.
      The Norwegian expedition that climbed the highest
point of the Hindu Kush (24, 623 ft.) in 1950. Ed.

702 NOWILL, Sidney Edward Payn
      The mountains of my life: journeys in Turkey and
the Alps / by "Ashenden" (pseud.). - Edinburgh, Blackwood, 1954. - 211 p. : plates.

703 NOYCE, Wilfred Cuthbert Francis
      The Alps / by Wilfred Noyce; with descriptive essays
by Karl Lukan; trans. from the German by Margaret
Shenfield. - London: Thames and Hudson, 1961. - 312
p. : 230 illus.
      Orig. pub. as Die Alpen von Mar Ventoux zum Kah-
buby, by Karl Lukan; Vienna: Scholl, 1959. A picture
book by leading European photographers. Ed.

704 _____ .
      Climber's fireside book / comp. by Wilfred Noyce. -
London: Heinemann, 1964. - 268 p. : 16 plates, 21 1/2 cm.
      An anthology carefully selected to include most of
the famous climbers from the early travelers to the modern heroes like Hillary and Bonington. Good combination of literary and technical writing. Ed.

705 _____ .
      Climbing the fishes' tail / by Wilfred Noyce. - Lon-
don: Heinemann, 1958. - 150 p. : 2 maps, 24 plates.
      An exciting and humorous but unsuccessful attempt
on Machapuchare--the sacred mountain. Ed.

706 _____ .
      Everest is climbed / by C. W. F. Noyce and Rich-
ard Taylor. - Harmondsworth: Penguin Books, 1954. -
30 p. : illus.
      Children's book.

707 _____ .
      Mountains and men / by Wilfred Noyce. - Rev. ed. -
London: Bles, 1954. - 160 p. : plates. First pub. 1947.
      An autobiography of the early climbing life of the
author. Ed.
      "The army bore him [the author] to India where, in

1943, he seized the opportunity of visiting Garhwal and
the approaches to Trisul.   Then he succeeded in the ascent of Pauhunri. " Yakushi.

708
        .
        Scholar mountaineers: pioneers of Parnassus, etc. /
by Wilfred Noyce. - London: Denis Dobson, 1950. -
164 p. : plates.
        A group of essays about 12 persons chosen for their
literary interpretation of mountains. Ed.

709
        .
        South Col: one man's adventure on the ascent of
Everest, 1953/ by Wilfred Noyce; foreword by Sir John
Hunt, line drawings by A. J. Veilhorn. - London:
Heinemann, 1954. - 145 p. : 16 plates, 3 maps. (New
Windmill series/ ed. by Ian Serraillier)

710
        .
        Springs of adventure/ by Wilfred Noyce. - 240 p. :
bibl.

711
        .
        They survived: a study of the will to live/ by Wil-
fred Noyce. - London: Heinemann, 1962. - 202 p. : ill. ,
12 plates, map, plan, bibl.
        Survival in the face of extreme physical hardship. Ed.

712
        .
        To the unknown mountain: ascent of an unexplored
25, 000 [foot mountain] in the Karakoram/ by Wilfred
Noyce. - London: Heinemann, 1962. - 183 p. : 3 maps,
12 plates.

713
        .
        World atlas of mountaineering/ ed. by W. Noyce
and Ian McMorrin. - London. Nelson, 1969. - 224 p. :
48 plates, illus. , 32 maps, 21 1/2 cm.
        An over extended book in scope but the ten contri-
butors manage to encompass most of the world with accounts of expeditions plus advice to novices. Ed.
        See also PYATT, Edward Charles (771); SUTTON,
Geoffrey (955); YOUNG, Geoffrey Winthrop (1131)

714 NUNLIST, Hugo
        Spitzbergen: the story of the 1962 Swiss-Spitzbergen
Expedition/ by Hugo Nunlist: trans. from the German

by Oliver Coburn. - New York: Barnes, 1966. - 191
p. : 24 plates.
A team of Swiss climbers cheerfully climbed many
new peaks in this forgotten area. Written in a clear,
compact style both vivid and informative. Ed.

715 ODELL, Noel C.
Nanda Devi/ by Noel C. Odell. - 1936.

716 O'KANE, Walter Collins
Trails and summits of the Adirondacks/ by Walter
C. O'Kane. - Boston: Houghton Mifflin, 1928. - 330 p. :
ill. (Riverside outdoor handbooks)
A tramper's and walker's detailed guide to the Adirondack mountains; peripherally of mountaineering interest. Ed.

717 _____.
Trails and summits of the White Mountains/ by
Walter C. O'Kane. - Boston: Houghton Mifflin, 1925. -
308 p. : ill. , plates. (Riverside outdoor handbooks)
A manual of mountain climbing for beginners and
climbers which answers the question "why climb?" Includes a guide to 19 one-day climbs. Ed.

718 OLSEN, Jack
The climb up to hell/ by Jack Olsen; with an intro.
by Christopher Brasher. - London: Gollancz, 1962. -
191 p. : 26 plates, diagr.
Thrilling rescue on the Eiger. Ed.

719 OLUFSEN, O.
Through the unknown Pamirs: the Second Danish
Pamir Expedition, 1898-99. - London: Heinemann,
1904. - 2 vols.

720 OPPENHEIM, E. C.
New climbs in Norway: an account of some ascents
in the Sondmore District/ by E. C. Oppenheim, ill. by
A. D. McCormick and from photographs. - London:
Allen & Unwin, 1898. - 257 p.

721 _____.
Some peaks/ by E. C. Oppenheim. - London: Unwin, 1898.

722 ORLOB, Helen
Mountain rescue/ by Helen Orlob. - New York, Nel-

son, 1963. - 176 p. : ill. , ports.
Children's book.

ORMEROD, Alick see WHILLANS, Don (1071)

723   OSMASTON, Henry Arthur
Guide to the Ruwenzori: the Mountains of the Moon /
by H. A. Osmaston and D. Pasteur.   - Uganda: Mountain Club of Uganda, Goring, West Col. Productions,
1972.   - 200 p. : ill. , (1col.) map.

724   OUTRAM, Sir James
In the heart of the Canadian Rockies / by Sir James
Outram.   - New York: Macmillan, 1905.   - xii, 466 p.
A chronicle of a score of first ascents in the Canadian Rockies, written with enthusiasm, which succeeds
in displacing the European Alps in the minds of American climbers. Ed.

725   OWEN, Jesse Coleman
Southern mountaineers / by J. C. Owen.   - Spartan-
burg, S. C. :   1952.   - 65 p. : ill.

726   PACKARD, Alpheus Spring
Ascent of the volcano of Popocateptl / by A. S.
Packard.   - (S. L.):   1886.

727   PACKE, Charles
A guide to the Pyrenees: especially intended for
the use of mountaineers / by C. Packe.   - 2nd ed. re-
written and much enlarged.   - London: 1867.   - diagrs. ,
maps, tables.   First pub. 1862.

728   PALLIS, Marco
Peaks and lamas: descriptions of travel on the bor-
der of India and Tibet, with a section on Tibetan art /
by Marco Pallis.   - London: Cassell, 1939.   - xx, 428 p.
Climbing in the Himalayas, together with a study of
Tibetan Buddhism and information on Tibetan art and
life. Ed.

729   PALMER, Howard S.
Edward W. D. Holway: a pioneer of the Canadian
Alps / by Howard S. Palmer.   - Minneapolis: University
of Minnesota Press, 1931.   - 81 p. : plates, part.

730   _____ .
Mountaineering and exploration on the Selkirks: a

record of pioneer work among the Canadian Alps, 1908-1912/ by Howard S. Palmer. - London: Putnam, 1914. 439 p. : 219 ill. , 2 maps.

731 _____ .
The Rocky mountains of Canada/ by Howard S. Palmer and J. Monroe Thorington. - New York: American Alpine Club, 1940.

732 PALMER, William Thomas
The complete hill walker, rock climber and cave explorer/ by W. T. Palmer. - London: Pitman, 1934. - 219 p.
Describes the techniques and problems of rockclimbing as a sport for the amateur and average hiker with a definite practical use for English walkers. Ed.

733 _____ .
English lakes: their topographical, historical and literary landmarks/ by William Thomas Palmer. - London: Harrap, 1932. - 281 p. : ill.
Contains practical information for the climber or hiker in lakeland by a former editor of the Fell and Rock Climbing Club. Ed.

734 _____ .
Odd corners in English lakeland: rambles, scrambles, climbs and sports/ by W. T. Palmer. - London: Skeffington & Son, 1913. - viii, 186 p. : 15 ill.

735 _____ .
Odd corners in the Yorkshire dales: rambles, scrambles, climbs and sports/ by W. T. Palmer. - London: Skeffington & Son, 1937. - 224 p. : plates.

736 PARKER, Herschel C.
Climbs on gritstone/ ed. by H. C. Parker. - Birkenhead, Willmer Bros. , 1948. - 3v. Vol. 1 under title, Laddow Area.
See also BROWNE, Belmore (131)

737 PASCOE, John Dobree
Great days in New Zealand mountaineering/ by John Dobree Pascoe; with a foreword by Sir Edmund Hillary. - London: Bailey & Swinfen, 1958. - 199 p. : front, 16 plates, maps, bibl.
Also pub. Wellington, N. Z. : Reed, 1958.

738
Land uplifted high: on the highlands of New Zealand / by J. D. Pascoe. - Christchurch, N. Z. : Whitcombe and Tombs, 1952. - 228 p. : plates.

739
Mountains, the bush and the sea: a photographic report / by John Dobree Pascoe. - Christchurch: Whitcombe & Tombs, 1950. - 96 plates.

740
Unclimbed New Zealand: Alpine travel in the Canterbury and Westland Ranges - Southern Alps / by John Dobree Pascoe. - London: Allen & Unwin, 1939. - 238 p. : 78 ill. , 2 sketches, 3 maps.
Gives an excellent notion of the strenuousness of mountaineering in New Zealand--bushwalking, bivouacking and carrying 60-70 lb. loads. Ed.

PASTEUR, D.   see   OSMASTON, Henry Arthur (723)

741   PATERSON, M.
Mountaineering below the snow line: or the solitary pedestrian in Snowdonia and elsewhere / by M. Paterson, with etchings by Mackaness. - London: G. Redway, 1886. - viii, 307 p. . ill.

742   PATEY, Tom
One man's mountains: essays and verses / by Tom Patey; foreword by Christopher Brasher. - London: Gollancz, 1971. - 287 p. : 23 plates, ill. , ports.
A literary collection of articles by the author of climbing stories in Britain since 1950. Interesting reading. Ed.

743   PATTERDALE MOUNTAIN RESCUE ASSOCIATION
Annual reports. - (S. L.): the association, 1905.

744   PAULCKE, Wilhelm
Hazards in mountaineering / by W. Paulcke and Dumler; trans. from the German by E. Noel Bowman. - London: Kaye and Ward, 1973. - 161 p. : Glossary, plates, bibl.
A modern, comprehensive summary of hazards with emphasis on avalanches. Good photography but of limited rock climbing interest. Ed.

745 PAUSE, Walter
Salute the mountains: the hundred best walks in the
Alps/ by Walter Pause, trans. from the German by
Ruth Michaelis-Jeng and Arthur Ratcliff. - London:
Harrap, 1962. - 211 p. : ill. , maps.
First pub. as Berg heil; Munich: Bayerische Land-
wirtschaft, 1955.

746 PEACOCKE, Thomas Arthur Hardy
Mountaineering/ by T. A. H. Peacocke. - 3rd ed. -
London: Black, 1954. - 212 p. : 13 ill. , plates, 18 1/2
cm. First pub. 1941. (the sportsman's library)
For the beginner generally; simple, direct and sound
(as of 1954) in covering most aspects of the subject. Ed.

747 PECK, Annie S.
High mountain climbing in Peru and Bolivia: a
search for the apex of America, including the conquest
of Huascaran; with some observations of the country and
people below/ by A. S. Peck. - London: Fisher and
Unwin, 1912. - 370 p. : ill.
One of the first major peaks of the world climbed
by a woman. Also pub. New York, 1911, as A search
for the apex of America. Ed.

748 PERCIVAL, Walter
Mountain memories/ by Walter Percival. - London:
1962. - 120 p.

749 PERRY, Alexander W.
Welsh mountaineering: a practical guide/ by Alexander W. Perry. - London: L. Upcott Gill, 1896. -
172 p.

750 PETZOLDT, Patricia
On top of the world: my adventures with my moun-
tain-climbing husband/ by Patricia Petzoldt. - London:
Collins, 1954. - 253 p. : plates.
The story of her husband's life, some shared experiences and some second hand. Starts with a wandering near-hobo youth climbing in the Tetons, Alps, Himalayas, South America and finally ends with homesteading
in Wyoming. Ed.

751 PICKMAN, Dudley Leavitt
Some mountain views/ by Dudley Leavitt Pickman. -
Boston: Manthorne & Co. , 1934. - 94 p. : ill.

A light, informal book containing reminiscences of mountain climbing and scenery in many parts of the globe dating back to 1875. Ed.

752   PIERRE, Bernard
         Mountain called Nun Kun: the Franco-Indian expedition to Nun Kun / by B. Pierre; trans. from the French by Nea Morin and Janet Adam Smith. - London: Hodder & Stoughton, 1955. - 189 p. : 16 plates, maps, 20 1/2 cm.
         Orig. pub. as Une Montagne nommée Nun Kun; Paris, Amiot-Dumest. Account of the 1953 French-Indian expedition that effected the first ascent of the Nun. Claude Kogan and P. Vitoz reached the summit. Ed.

753   PIGGOTT, Percy J.
         Burrow's guide to North Wales (British Holidays in North Wales) with a special article upon mountain walks and rock climbs by Mrs. Dora Benson. - London: Burrow, 1919.
         Various eds.

754   _____.
         Burrow's guide to the Lake District; a practical handbook for the tourist with a special article upon mountain passes, walks and rock climbs, by Mrs. Dora Benson. - London: Burrow, 1920.
         Various eds.

755   PILDITCH, Sir Philip Harold
         Uphill journey / by John Bartropp (pseud.). - London: Chambers, 1938. - 319 p.

756   PILKINGTON, Charles
         Climbing without guides / by Charles Pilkington. - Leeds: 1897. The conclusion of a lecture to the Yorkshire Ramblers Club, 27 October 1890. Ed.

PILLEY, Dorothy see RICHARDS, Dorothy E. (795)

PINKERTON, John see RAMOND de CARBONNIERES: Louis François Elizabeth (778)

756a   PINKERTON'S VOYAGES AND TRAVELS: Volume IV
         Contents: Saussure's attempts to reach the summit of Mont Blanc. Raymond's journey to the summit of Mont Perdu.

PIUS XI, Pope see RATTI, Abate Achille (781); GAS-
QUET, Francis Aidan (355)

757 PLATT, W.
The joy of mountains/ W. Platt. - (S. L.): Bell,
1921. - 78 p.

758 PLUNKET, Frederica Louisa Edith
Here and there among the Alps/ by F. Plunket. -
London: Longmans, 1875. - 195 p.

759 PLYMIRE, John David
High adventure in Tibet/ by John David. - Spring-
field: Gospel Pub. House, 1959. - 225 p. : ill.

760 PORTER, Edward C.
Library of mountaineering and exploration and travel; both true and in fiction, science, technique, philosophy, art/ by Edward C. Porter. - Chicago, 1959. -
74 p. : 2 plates. 750 titles listed.

761 POUCHER, William Arthur
Climbing with a camera: the Lake District/ by W.
A. Poucher. - London: Country Life, 1963. - 108 p. : ill.

762 _____.
The Scottish peaks: a pictorial guide to walking in
this region and to the safe ascent of its most spectacular
mountains/ by William Arthur Poucher. - London: Constable, 1964. - 422 p. : front. , 199 ill. , 31 maps, tables,
diagrs.

763 POWELL, Paul Sidney
Just where do you think you've been?/ by Paul Powell. - Wellington, N. Z. : Reed, 211 p. : ill. , maps.
An autobiographical series of sketches which illus-
trates the unique nature of New Zealand climbing. Ed.

764 _____.
Men aspiring/ by Paul Powell. - Wellington, N. Z. :
Reed, 1967. - 183 p. : ill. , maps.
A personal life-long relationship with a mountain
which combines insight into the motivation of climbers
plus a history of this New Zealand peak. Ed.

POWNALL, Dick see CASEWIT, Curtis W. (162)

765 PRAG, P.
Mountain holidays in Norway/ comp. by P. Prag. -
Oslo: Norway Travel Association, 1963.

766 PRINGLE, Sir John
A discourse on the attraction of mountains: deliver-
ed at the anniversary meeting of the Royal Society, Nov-
embeɪ, 1775/ by Sir John Pringle. - London: the Royal
Society, 1775.

767 PRINGLE, M. A.
Towards the Mountains of the Moon/ by M. A.
Pringle. - London: 1884.

768 PRIOR, Herman
Guide to the Lake District of England/ by Herman
Prior. - 7th ed. Windermere: J. Garnett, 1890. - xi,
448 p.
Previous ed. title varies: Ascents and passes in
the Lake District of England: being a new pedestrian
and general guide to the district/ and, Pedestrian and
general guide to the Lake District of England/ 2nd ed. -
255 p.

769 PUBLIC SCHOOLS ALPINE SPORTS CLUB
Winter sports and mountaineering: bibliography/
comp. by the Public Schools Alpine Sports Club. - 3rd
ed. - London: National Book Council, 1928. - (Bibliography, No. 30)

770 PYATT, Edward Charles
The Boy's book of mountains and mountaineering/
by Edward Charles Pyatt. - London: Burke, 1963. -
144 p. : ill. , map, facsim. , diagr.

771   .
_____ British crags and climbers; an anthology/ by E. C.
Pyatt and W. Noyce. - London: Dobson Pub. , 1952. -
235 p. : plates.
Anthology devoted to climbing in England compiled
from books and club journals; takes in the main districts,
and oddments like Beachy Head, Dartmoor and Cornwall.
Many classic first ascents. Ed.

772   .
_____ A climber in the West Country/ by E. C. Pyatt. -

Newton Abbott: David & Charles, 1968. - 204 p. : 21 ill. , 2 maps, ports, bibl.

773 _____ .
Climbing and walking in south-east England / by E. C. Pyatt. - David and Charles, 1970. - 173 p. : ill, 2 maps.

774 _____ .
Mountains of Britain / by E. C. Pyatt. - London: Batsford, 1966. - 216 p. : ill. , (same ed.), 11 maps. (Britain series)

775 _____ .
Where to climb in the British Isles / by E. C. Pyatt. - London: Faber, 1960.
It is a work of order and precision with a fresh, unbiased approach, based on personal experience. It would be useful when planning a long holiday and even more valuable to the weekend visitor to the cliffs and outcrops. It tells how to get there. Ed.
See also CLARK, Ronald William (188)

776 PYE, David
George Leigh Mallory / by David Pye. - London: Oxford University Press, 1927.
A memoir by a climbing friend of the outstanding mountaineer who was lost on Everest in 1920. Ed.

777 RAEBURN, Harold
Mountaineering art / by Harold Raeburn; with diagrams and illustrations. - London: Fisher Unwin, 1920. - 274 p.
A technical book of technique from bouldering to conquering the highest summits; written as a compendium of all the skill and knowledge in mountaineering available in 1920. A classic instruction manual. Ed.

778 RAMOND de CARBONNIERES, Louis François Elizabeth
Journey to the summit of Mont-Perdu, the highest mountain in the Pyrenees / by Ramond de Carbonnières.
Vol. IV of A general collection of the best and most interesting voyages and travels in all parts of the world; many of which are now first translated into English / ed. by John Pinkerton. - London: 1808-14. - 17v. : plates.

779 _____ .
Travels in the Pyrenees / by Ramond de Carbonn-

ières; trans. from the French by F. Gold. - London:
1813.

780 RAND, Christopher
     Mountains and water / by C. Rand. - London: Ox-
ford University Press, 1965.
     The New Yorker's former "reporter at large" inves-
tigates some of the best known parts of the world and
makes them come alive. Ed.

781 RATTI, Achille, Pope Pius XI
     Climbs on alpine peaks / by Pope Pius XI, with a
foreword by Douglas Freshfield, intro. by L. C. Casar-
telli and trans. by J. E. C. Eaton. - London: Fisher
and Unwin, 1923. - 136 p. : plates, port.
     Written with moderation and accuracy and charm.
Describes ascents of Monte Rosa, Matterhorn and Mont
Blanc. Well worth reading even if the author had re-
mained anonymous. Ed.
     See also GASQUET, Francis Aidan (355)

781a RAWSON, Henry Anthony
     What makes a team? / by Henry Anthony Rawson. -
London: Newman Neame Take Home Books, 1956. - 15 p.
On teamwork in sport and mountaineering. Ed.

782 READE, J. V.
     Some Oberland climbs in 1907 / by J. Reade. - Lon-
don: 1908.

783 REASON, Joyce
     Heights after Everest: Howard Somervell of India /
By Joyce Reason. - London: Edinburgh House Pr. ,
1954. - 24 p.

784 REBUFFET, Gaston
     Between heaven and earth / by G. Rebuffet and
Pierre Tarroz; trans. from the French by Eleanor Brockett. - London: Kaye and Ward, 1970. - 183 p. : 8
plates, ill. , ports.
     First pub. 1965. Sheer mountaineering inspiration
with plates and text from an award winning film at the
Cannes Film Festival. Ed.

785 _____ .
     Men and the Matterhorn: experiences of the author
and others on the Matterhorn / by Gaston Rebuffet; trans.
from the French by Eleanor Brockett. - London: Nicho-

las Vane, 1967. - 222 p. : 118 ill. , (23 col)
Orig. pub. Paris: Hachette, 1965. The definitive
book on the Matterhorn; recreates history before the
reader's eyes. Makes other Matterhorn books pale by
comparison. Ed.

786 _____ .
Mont Blanc to Everest/ by Gaston Rebuffet; trans.
from the French by Geoffrey Sutton. Captions by Wilfred Noyce. - London: Thames and Hudson, 1956. -
158 p. : 69 ill. (8 col.)
First pub. as De Mont Blanc à Himalay; Grenoble:
Arthaud, 1955. Marvelous book of illustrations with a
short text tracing the history of mountaineering. Lyri-
cal photographs. Ed.

787 _____ .
On ice and snow and rock/ by G. Rebuffat; trans.
from the French by Patrick Evans. - London: Kaye
and Ward, 1971. - 191 p. : ill. , ports.
Rev. ed. of On Snow and rock (788); still the most
inspiring manual of climbing, with numerous photographs
illustrating technique. Ed.

788 _____ .
On snow and rock/ by Gaston Rebuffet, trans. from
the French by Geoffrey Sutton. - (2nd ed.) London:
Kaye and Ward, 1967. - 192 p. : plates, 22 1/1 cm.
Orig. pub. Paris, 1959; first ed. trans. by Eleanor
Brockett with technical assistance from J. E. B. Wright,
1963. A book of plates illustrating climbing technique
in the French Alps: superb photography and detailed
text. Ed.

789 _____ .
Starlight and storm/ by Gaston Rebuffet; trans. from
the French. - London: Kaye & Ward, 1968. - 224 p. :
plates.
Sheer poetry in photography and expression, this is
one of the author's early books but is a classic model
of alpine writing. Ed.

790 RECLUS, Elisée
History of a mountain/ by E. Reclus, trans. by
Bertha Ness and John Lillie, 1881.

791 REID, Mayne
The Cliff-climbers: or, the lone home in the Hima-

layas; a sequel to the plant-hunters/ by Captain Mayne
Reid. - Boston: 1864. - 304 p. : ill.

792 REY, Guido
      The Matterhorn/ by Guido Rey; with an intro. by
Edmondo de Amicis; trans. from the Italian by J. E. C.
Eaton. Rev. by R. L. G. Irving. - Oxford: Blackwell,
1949. - 278 p. : plates, ill , port.
      First pub. London: Fisher and Unwin, 1907. A
history of climbs on the Matterhorn including the author's remarkable exploits. Ed.

793   .
      Peaks and precipices: scrambles in the Dolomites
and Savoy/ by G. Rey. - London: 1914.

794 RICHARD, Colette
      Climbing blind/ by Colette Richard; trans. from the
French by Norman Dale, with a foreword by Maurice
Herzog and a preface by Norbert Casteret. - London:
Hodder & Stoughton, 1966. - 159 p. : 4 plates.
      Worthwhile reading of the successes of a blind wo-
man climbing major peaks in Europe: includes chapters
on speleology. Ed.

795 RICHARDS, Dorothy E.
      Climbing days: autobiographical reminiscences/ by
Dorothy E. Richards. - London: Bell, 1935. - 352 p. :
plates.
      Good climbs at home and in the Alps, described
with engaging frankness and enthusiasm by a humane and
humorous climber. Ed.

796 RICHMOND, William Kenneth
      Climber's testament/ by William Kenneth Richmond. -
[S. L]: Redman, 1950. 246p. ; 36 pl.

797 RICKMERS, Willi Gustav Rickmer
      Skiing for beginners and mountaineers ... / by W.
G. R. Rickmers; with photographs by A. Hacker and
silhouettes by Elsa von Lepkowski. - London: Fisher
and Unwin, 1910. - 175 p.

798 RITCHIE, John
      List of books in the English language on travel, ex-
ploration and mountaineering published within the year
ending August thirty-first, 1897/ by John Ritchie. -
Boston: Boston Scientific Society, 1897. - 18 p. : (Oc-

casional publication, No. 2)

799 ROBBINS, Leonard Harman
      Mountains and men / by Leonard Harman Robbins. -
      New York: Dodd, 1931. - 324 p. : ill. , plates, map.
      The most comprehensive book on mountain climbing
      as of 1931; contains accounts of great ascents and fail-
      ures in admirable style. Ed.

800 ROBBINS, Royal
      Advanced rockcraft / by Royal Robbins. - Glendale,
      Calif. : La Siesta Press, 1975. - ill.
      A continuation of the author's Basic Rockcraft (800a);
      a very clear and entertaining manual. Leaves an ex-
      perienced climber feeling that there must be more that
      can be written at the advanced level. Ed.

800a _____.
      Basic rockcraft / by Royal Robbins, ill. , by Sheri-
      dan Anderson. - Glendale, Calif. : La Siesta Press,
      1971. - 71 p. : ill. , plates.
      One of the clearest instruction manuals yet printed
      though lacking in detail. The illustrations are entertain-
      ing; definitely recommended for all climbers. Ed.

801 ROBERTS, A. R.
      Himalayan holiday: an account of the New Zealand
      Himalayan expedition 1953 / by A. R. Roberts and
      others. - Christchurch: Whitcombe & Tombs, 1954. -
      44 p. : ill. , map.
      This pamphlet is the endeavour of a group of New
      Zealand climbers to tell their fellows of a private ex-
      pedition to Ganesh Himal and Sringi Himal in the Cen-
      tral Nepal Himalaya.   They made the first ascent of
      Chamar, 7177 meters high. Ed.

802 ROBERTS, David
      Deborah: a mountain wilderness / by David Roberts. -
      New York: Vanguard, 1970. - 180 p. : 15 ill. , 3 maps.
      Personal experiences of D. Roberts and D. Jenssen
      while mountain climbing in Alaska in the summer of
      1964. Ed.

803 _____.
      The mountain of my fear / by David Roberts. - Lon-
      don: Souvenir, 1968. - 157 p. : 16 plates, ill. , maps,
      ports.

Ascent of the West face of Alaska's Mt. Huntington. Personal and emotional encounter with the mountain. Ed.

804　ROBERTS, Dennis
I'll climb Mt. Everest alone; the story of Maurice Wilson/ by Dennis Roberts. - London: Robert Hale, 1957. - 158 p. : 16 plates, maps, 21 1/2 cm.
This is the story of Captain M. Wilson, who undertook to climb Mount Everest alone on the basis of faith and fasting, and who ultimately perished at the foot of the North Col at 21,500 ft., in May, 1934. The author had access to Wilson's diaries and letters. Ed.

805　ROBERTS, Eric
Stubai Alps: a survey of popular walking and climbing routes/ comp. by Eric Roberts. - Goring, West Col Productions, 1972. - 156 p. : ill., maps.

806　ROBERTS, Morley
The western Avernus (or toil and travel in further North America: Canadian Rockies)/ by Morley Roberts. - London: Smith, Elder, 1887. - 207 p.

807　ROBERTSON, David
George Mallory/ by David Robertson. - London: Faber, 1969. - 279 p. : 16 plates, maps.
Full biography of Mallory, who disappeared on the way to the top of Mount Everest in 1924. Ed.

808　ROBERTSON, Maxwell
Mountain panorama: a book of winter sports and climbing/ by Max Robertson with contrib. by Sir John Hunt and others. - London: Max Parrish, 1955. - 128 p. : ill., plates.
This book includes an account of the attempt on Peak OC, Saltoro Kangri. Ed.

809　ROBINSON, Anthony M.
Alpine roundabout/ by Anthony M. Robinson. - London: Chapman & Hall, 1947. - 214 p. : plates.

810　ROBINSON, John
Camping and climbing in Baja [California]/ by John Robinson. - rev. ed. : La Siesta, 1971.

811　ROBSON, P.
Mountains of Kenya/ by P. Robson. - Nairobi: East African Pub. Co., 1969.

812 ROCH, Andre
  Climbs of my youth / by Andre Roch. - London:
Dent, 1956. - 159 p. : plates.
  First pub. , London: Lindsay Drummond, 1949.

813 _____.
  Everest 1952, etc. : photographs of the Swiss Expedition / by Andre Roch. - 110 p. : plates.

814 _____.
  On rock and ice: mountaineering in photographs /
by Andre Roch. - London: Adam & Charles Black,
1947. - 80 p.

815 ROCK-CLIMBING IN CUMBERLAND:
  A notebook for novices; via Furness Railway. -
n. p. : privately printed, 1913. - 43 p. : ill.

816 ROMM, Mikhail, D.
  Ascent of Mount Stalin / by Mikhail D. Romm; trans.
by Alec Brown. - London: Laurence and Wisehart,
1936. - 270 p. : plates, map.
  Mt. Stalin, presently Pik Communism, 7495 meters,
was discovered by Diemler and Rickmers in 1913. The
summit was ascended on September 3, 1933, by Abalakov
and Gorbounov. Ed.

ROSS, Francis Edward see BAKER, Ernest Albert (46)

817 ROSS, J. L.
  A selected list on mountaineering / ed. by J. L.
Ross. - Glasgow: Corporation Public Libraries, 1951. -
15 p.
  A list of approximately 100 titles with locations
within the Glasgow Public Libraries, some entries are
accompanied by a brief description. Ed.

818 ROSS, Malcolm
  Aorangi: or the heart of the Southern Alps, New
Zealand / by Malcolm Ross.

819 _____.
  Climber in New Zealand / by Malcolm Ross; illus.
from photographs by the author; with a prefatory note
by Viscount Bryce. - London: Edward Arnold, 1914. -
316 p. : plates.

820 ROSSIT, Edward A.
Northwest mountaineering/ by Edward A. Rossit. -
Caldwell, Idaho: Caxton Printers, 1965. - 206 p. : ill.

821 _____.
Snow camping and mountaineering/ by Edward A.
Rossit; illus. by Charles P. Conley. - New York, Funk
and Wagnalls, 1970. - 276 p. : ill.

822 ROWLAND, Edward George
The ascent of Snowden/ by Edward George Rowland;
foreword by John Disley, ill. by Jonah Jones. - Pentre-
felin, Criccieth: Cidron Press, 1956. - 21 p. : map.

823 ROYAL GEOGRAPHICAL SOCIETY
Everest: a guide to the climb/ by the Royal Geo-
graphical Society and Alpine Club. Joint Himalayan
Committee. - 1955. - map.

ROYLE, B. see MELDRUM, Kim (608)

824 RUCKSACK CLUB
Catalogue of books in the Rucksack Club's Library
located in the Manchester Corporation central library. -
Manchester: Rucksack Club, 1954. - 24 p.

825 RUDGE, E. C. W.
Mountain days near home/ by E. C. W. Rudge. -
n. p. : privately printed, 1941. - 76 p. : ill.

826 RUMNEY, A. W.
The way about the English Lake District: with appendices on crag climbing/ by A. W. Rumney. - 160 p.

827 RUSK, C. E.
Tales of a western mountaineer: record of moun-
tain experiences on the Pacific Coast/ by C. D. Rusk -
Boston: Houghton Mifflin, 1924. - xii, 309 p. : ill.

828 RUSSELL, Jean
Climb if you will: a commentary on Geoff Hayes
and his club, the Oread Mountaineering Club/ comp. and
ed. by Jean Russell, in association with Jack Ashcroft
... (et al.). - Ashbourne: EXPO 4974, 1974. - 222 p. :
ill. , ports, 22 cm.

829 RUSSELL, R. Scott
Mountain prospect/ by R. Scott Russell. - London:

Chatto & Windus, 1946. - 247 p. : plates, maps, 20 1/2 cm.
Climbs in New Zealand, Jan Mayen Island and the
Karakoram; extremely well written. Ed.

830   RUTTLEDGE, Hugh
Attack on Everest / by Hugh Ruttledge. - n. p. : Mc-
Bride, 1935. - 339 p. : ill., map.
Also pub. under title: Everest, 1933. Account of the
unsuccessful 1933 expedition quite detailed, but written
with restraint and understatement. Ed.

831   _____.
Everest: the unfinished adventure / by Hugh Ruttledge. - London: Hodder & Stoughton, 1937. - 295 p. :
63 plates.

832   _____.
Everest 1933: an account of the 1933 Mount Everest
Expedition / by Hugh Ruttledge. - London: Hodder &
Stoughton, 1934. - 390 p. : 59 plates, ports, maps.

833   SACK, John
Ascent of Yerupaga / by John Sack. - London: Herbert Jenkins, 1954. - 191 p. : plates, map, 19 1/2 cm.

834   _____.
The butcher: the ascent of Yerapuja / by John
Sack. - New York: Holt, Rinehart & Winston, 1952. -
213 p. : ill.
The author was the only non-climber among seven
American college boys who conquered the then highest
unclimbed mountain in the Western hemisphere. A
lighthearted, non-technical description that falls far below the action described. Ed.

835   SAMUEL, Herbert L.
Man of action, man of the spirit: Sir Francis
Younghusband / Herbert L. Samuel. - London: World
Congress of Faiths, 1953. - 8 p.

836   SANDEMAN, R. G.
Mountaineer's journal / by R. G. Sandeman. - Car-
marthen: Druid, 1948. - 168 p. : plates.
Deals with the less well-known climbs on Brecon
Beacons and the Cairngorms in snow and ice conditions. Ed.

837   SANUKI, M.
The Alps / by M. Sanuki and K. Yamada. - London:

World book, 1970. - 146 p. : col. ill. , maps, col. port.

SAUSSURE, Horace Benedict de see FRESHFIELD,
    Douglas William (346)

838   SAYRE, Woodrow Wilson
      Four against Everest/ by Woodrow Wilson Sayre. -
London: Baker 1964. - 251 p. : ill. , ports, maps,
tables, 22 1/2 cm.
      Unsuccessful attempt by four men to reach the sum-
mit of Mt. Everest without permission of the authorities,
Sherpas or oxygen. By a professor of philosophy with
meditations on the philosophy of mountain climbing. Ed.

SAYWARD, Perceval see BENT, Allen Herbert (86)

839   SCANLAN, A. B.
      Egmont: the story of a mountain/ by A. B. Scan-
lan. - Wellington, N. Z. : 1961. - 200 p. : ill. , 3 maps.
      "Legends, Maori tribal history, exploration and as-
cent. " Dawson's.

840   SCARR, Josephine
      Four miles high/ Josephine Scarr. - London: Gol-
lancz, 1966. - 188 p. : maps, plates.
      The Women's Kulu Expedition, demonstrating the
equality of the sexes, in which no obstacle was too difficult to tackle. Ed.

841   SCHOMBERG, Reginald Charles Francis
      Kafirs and glaciers: travels in Chitral/ by R. C.
F. Schomberg. - London: Martin Hopkinson, 1938. -
287 p. : plates, map.

842
      Peaks and plains of central Asia/ by R. C. F.
Schomberg. - London: Hopkinson, 1933. - 000 p. : ill

843
      Unknown Karakorum/ by R. C. F. Schomberg. -
London: Martin Hopkinson, 1936. - 244 p. : plates, map.

844   SCHUSTER, Claud (1st Baron Schuster)
      Men, women and mountains: days in the Alps and
Pyrenees/ by Baron Schuster. - London: Nicholson &
Watson, 1931. - 143 p. : plates (ports.)

845
　　　.
　　　Mountaineering: the Romanes lecture 21st May, 1948/ by Baron Schuster. - London: Oxford University Press, 1948. - 32 p.

846
　　　.
　　　Peaks and pleasant pastures: papers on the Alps/ by Baron Schuster. - Oxford: Clarendon Press, 1911 - 227 p. : maps.

847
　　　.
　　　Postscript to adventure/ by Baron Schuster. - London: Eyre, 1950. - 214 p. : 8 plates, ill. (New Alpine library)

848 SCOTT, D. K.
　　　The Midlands Hindu Kush expedition, 1967/ by D. K. Scott and W. Cheverst. - Nottingham, Nottingham Climber's Club, 1968. - 62 p. : 41 pl., ill., ports., maps.

849 SCOTT, Doug
　　　Big wall climbing: development technique and aids/ by Doug Scott. - London: Kaye and Ward, 1974. - 320 p. : 200 pl., ill., maps. diagrs.
　　　Historical viewpoint plus basic and advanced techniques, for the armchair mountaineer, the weekend climber, as well as the more serious. Ed.

850 SCOTT, J. M.
　　　Gino Watkins/ by J. M. Scott. - 8th ed. - London: Hodder & Stoughton, 1951. - 352 p. : ill.

851 SCOTTISH MOUNTAINEERING CLUB GUIDE, 1920
　　　General guide-book, geology, meteorology, botany, bird life, equipment, maps, etc., rock and snow craft, photography/ Scottish Mountaineering Club. - Edinburgh: The Club, 1920. - plates.

852 SEAVER, George
　　　Francis Younghusband: explorer and mystic/ by George Seaver. - London: John Murray, 1952. - 391 p. : ill., maps.
　　　"Biography of Younghusband, who died in 1942....
He was President of the Royal Geographical Society and Chairman of the Mount Everest Committee. " Yakushi.

853 SELLA, Vittorio
    Catalogue of photographs ... taken during the tour
of Kanchinjinga made in 1899 by Mr. D. W. Freshfield/
by V. Sella and Edmund J. Garwood. - London: Spottiswoode, 1900. - 24 p.
    See also CLARK, Ronald William (191)

054 SERRAILLIER, Ian
    Everest climbed/ by Ian Serraillier. - 60 p. - Lon-
don: Oxford University Press, 1955.
    "Anthology and poem celebrating the ascent of Mount
Everest in 1953. " Yakushi.

855 _____.
    Mountain rescue/ by Ian Serraillier. - London:
Heinemann, 1955. - 149 p. : ill.
    Retold from Flight to adventure, a children's book.

856 SETON-KARR, Heywood W.
    Ten years travel and sport in foreign lands/ by H.
W. Seton-Karr. - 2nd Ed. - London: Chapman, 1890. -
445 p.

857 SHERMAN, Patrick
    Cloud-walkers: six climbs on major Canadian peaks/
by Paddy Sherman. - London: Macmillan, 1966. - 161
p. : front 16 plates, maps.
    Includes a chapter on Mt. Fairweather in Alaska.

858 SHERRING, Charles Atmore
    Western Tibet and the British Borderland ... with
an account of the government, religion and customs of
its people ... / by Charles A. Sherring; with a chapter
by T. G. Longstaff ... describing an attempt to climb
Gurla Mandhata. - London: Edward Arnold, 1906. -
376 p. : ill., maps.

859 SHIPTON, Eric Earle
    Blank on the map/ by Eric Shipton. - Hodder &
Stoughton, 1938. - 299 p. : plates, maps.
    An account of an expedition in the Karakorum Range.
Ed.

860 _____.
    Land of tempest: travels in Patagonia, 1958-62/ by
Eric Shipton. - London: Hodder & Stoughton, 1963. -

224 p. : 16 plates, 3 maps.
Captures the emotional aspect as well, in this part of his autobiography. Ed.

861 _____.
The Mt. Everest reconnaissance expedition, 1951/ by Eric Shipton. - London: Hodder & Stoughton, 1952. - 128 p. : ill. , maps, 92 plates.
By a veteran of four Everest expeditions, this book gives a brief account of the reconnaissance; over half the book is pictures. Ed.

862 _____.
Mountains of Tartary/ by Eric Shipton. - London: Hodder & Stoughton, 1951. - 224 p. : plates.
"Climbs and journeys in the Pamirs and Central Asia ... from 1940-1942 and 1946-1948. "

863 _____.
Nanda Devi/ by Eric Shipton, with a foreword by Hugh Ruttledge. - London: Hodder & Stoughton, 1936. - 310 p. : plates, 22 cm.
Exploration of the Nanda Devi sanctuary in 1934 by Shipton, Tilman and a handful of porters. Revelation of what a small, light expedition could achieve. Ed.

864 _____.
That intravelled world: an autobiography/ by Eric Shipton; illus. by BIRO. - London: Hodder & Stoughton, 1969. - 286 p. : ill. , maps, 16 plates.
More mountain exploration than climbing. Ed.

865 _____.
True book about Everest/ by Eric Shipton; ill. by R. Stocks May. - London: Muller, 1955. - 142 p.
For children.

866 _____.
Upon that mountain/ by Eric Shipton, with a foreword by Geoffrey Winthrop Young. - London: Hodder & Stoughton, 1943. - 222 p. : plates, maps, 20 cm.
Shipton's mountaineering career, Alps, East Africa (second ascent of Mt. Kenya with Tilman, Ruwenzori), Everest (four times), Nanda Devi and Karakoram. Ed.
See also HORIZON, New York (449)

867 A SHORT ACCOUNT OF MONT BLANC/ London: 1817.

SHUTTLEWORTH, F. see BURNS, W. C. (149a)

868 SIMONOV, Yevgeny
Conquering the Celestial Mountains/ by Yevgeny
Simonov. - Moscow: Foreign Language Pub. House,
1958. - 130 p. : ill.
"Account of the first ascent of Mustagh Ato." Yakushi.

SINGH, Gyan see GYAN SINGH (392)

869 SINIGAGLIA, Leone
Climbing reminiscences in the Dolomites/ by Leone
Sinigaglia; with an intro. by Edmund J. Garwood; trans.
by M. A. Vialls. - London: Fisher Unwin, 1896. - 224
p. : map, ill.

870 SKOCZYLAS, Adam
Stefano: we shall come tomorrow/ by Adam Skoczylas. - London: Poets and Painters Press, 1962. -
35 p. : 10 plates.
A rescue on Eiger 1957. Ed.

871 SLESSAR, Malcolm
The Andes are prickly/ by Malcolm Slessar. - London: Gollancz, 1966. - 254 p. : front 28 plates, maps.

872   .
Red Peak: a personal account of the British-Soviet
Pamir Expedition, 1962/ by Malcolm Slessar. - London:
Hodder & Stoughton, 1964. - 256 p. : 20 plates, map,
22 cm.
An account of a joint expedition by members of the
Alpine Club and the Scottish Alpine Club and a group of
expert Russian climbers. Includes the death of Wilfred
Noyce and Robin Smith. Ed.

873 SLINGSBY, William Cecil
Norway, the northern playground: sketches of climbing and mountain exploration in Norway between 1872 and
1903/ ed. by Eleanor Slingsby with biographical note by
Geoffrey Winthrop Young. - 2nd ed. - Oxford: Basil
Blackwell, 1941. - 227 p. : ill. , plates, map, 20 cm.
(Blackwells Mountaineering Library, vol. 7)
First pub. , Edinburgh: David Douglas, 1904. Friend
of Mummery, father-in-law of Winthrop Young--first
mountaineer to explore Norway, where he became some-
thing of a legend. Ed.

SMATKO, A. J.   see   VOGE, Harvey H. (1041)

874   SMEETON, Miles
       A taste of the hills / by Miles Smeeton. - London:
R. Hart-Davis, 1961. - 207 p. : ill. , maps, 21 1/2 cm.
       "Including a short account of the attempt to climb
Tirich Mir from Chitral. " Yakushi.

875   SMITH, Albert Richard
       A boy's ascent of Mont Blanc / by Albert Smith. -
London: 1860.

876   _____.
       A handbook of Mr. Albert Smith's ascent of Mont
Blanc / by Albert Smith. - London: 1852. - 28 p.
       "A nineteenth century account of the thrills and hor-
rors of the ascent with all the gruesome details. " RHB.

877   _____.
       The story of Mt. Blanc / by Albert Smith. - 2nd ed.
enl. - London: 1854.
       "Contains a record of his first ascent of Mt. Blanc
in 1851.... " RHB.
       See also THORINGTON, James Monroe (982)

878   SMITH, George Alan, ed.
       The armchair mountaineer: a gathering of wit, wis-
dom and idolatry / ed. by G. A. & Carol D. Smith. -
New York: Pitman, 1968. - 361 p. : ill.
       Historically based collection of anecdotes by Young,
Tyndale, Whymper; marred by absence of anything from
the last twenty years. Ed.

879   _____.
       Introduction to mountaineering / by George Alan Smith,
with intro. by James Ramsey Ullman. - New York:
Barnes, 1957.
       Reprint with intro. by James Ramsey Ullman. -
London: Yoseloff, 1960. - New rev. ed. - 1967. - 128
p. : ill. , 25 1/2 cm.

880   SMITH, James Buchanan Adam
       Mountaineering / by Janet Buchanan. - Cambridge: Uni-
versity Press, for the National Book League, 1955. -
24 p. : Reader's guides, second series, 1)
       A selected reading list with abstracts on each book--
a very good introduction to the subject. Ed.

881
_____.
Mountaineering holidays/ by Janet Smith. - London:
Dent, 1946. - 194 p. : 32 plates.
Aims at conveying the whole gamut of mountaineer-
ing holidays in the highlands and the Alps. Ed.

882 SMITH, Walter Percy Haskett
Climbing in the British Isles/ by Walter P. H.
Smith and H. C. Hart. - London: 1804 95. - 2v. Con-
tents: v. 1 England. v. 2, Wales and Ireland.

883
_____.
Home climbs/ by Walter P. H. Smith. - London:
1918.

884 SMITH, William
Adventures with my Alpen-stock and carpet-bag/ by
William Smith. - London: 1864.

885 SMYTHE, Frank Sydney
Adventures of a mountaineer/ by Frank Smythe. -
London: Dent, 1940. - 228 p. : 17 photos, ports. (Tra-
vellers tales)

886
_____.
Aguln Switzerland/ by Frank Smythe. - Hodder &
Stoughton, 1947. - 248 p. : plates.

887
_____.
Behold the mountains: climbing with a colour cam-
era/ by Frank Smythe. - London: Chanticleer, 1949. -
155 p. : 57 col. plates.
The blending of prose and pictures is superbly done,
in relating the author's experiences in all parts of the
world. Ed.

888
_____.
British mountaineers/ by Frank Smythe. - London:
Collins, 1942. - 47 p. : plates, ill. (Britain in pictures.
The British people in pictures).

889
_____.
A camera in the hills/ by Frank S. Smythe. - London: Black, 1940. - 147 p. : ill.

890
_____.
Camp six: an account of the 1933 Mount Everest

expedition/ by F. S. Smythe. - London: Hodder &
Stoughton, 1937. - 307 p. : plates, 23 cm.

891 _____ .
Climbs and ski runs/ by Frank S. Smythe. - Edinburgh: Blackwood, 1931.

891a _____ .
Climbs in the Canadian Rockies/ by Frank S.
Smythe. - London: Hodder & Stoughton, 1950. - 260
p. : plates, ill. , maps.
Exploration of the Lloyd George Range in British
Columbia and a number of ascents in the Canadian Na-
tional Park. Ed.

892 _____ .
Edward Whymper/ by Frank S. Smythe. - London:
Hodder & Stoughton, 1940. - 330 p. : plates, ports. , maps.
Though Whymper is forever identified with the Matterhorn, he lived for 45 years after that day of triumph
and disaster, explored in Spitzbergen and South America,
helped to open up the Rockies and quarrelled with most
other climbers. " NBL.

893 _____ .
Kamet conquered/ by Frank Smythe. - London:
Gollancz, 1932. - 420 p. : plates, 23 cm.
Also pub. Hodder & Stoughton, 1938. "Smythe led
a small British expedition to Kamet in Garhwol, which
became the first peak over 25,000 feet to be climbed. "
NBL.

894 _____ .
The Kanchenjunga adventure/ by Frank Smythe. -
London: Gollancz, 1930. - 464 p. : plates, 23 cm.
An account of the unsuccessful attempt of the party
led by Prof. Dyhrenfurth to climb Kanchenjunga. Ed.

895 _____ .
The mountain scene/ by F. S. Smythe, with seventy-
eight reproductions of photographs by the author. - London: Black, 1937. - 153 p. : ill. , plates, 28 cm.

896 _____ .
The mountain top/ by Frank S. Smythe. - London:
St. Hughes Press, 1947. - 45 p.

897 _____ .
Mountain Vision/ by Frank S. Smythe. - London:

Hodder & Stoughton, 1941. - 308 p. : plates.

897a _____.
Mountaineering and skiing in the Alps, Gt. Britain
and Corsica / by Frank S. Smythe; with a foreword by
Geoffrey Winthrop Young. - New ed. London: Black,
1957. - 197 p. : 7 plates.
Includes storm on the Shreckhorn and the first as-
cent of the west buttress of Clogwyn dur Arddu behind
Jack Langland. Ed.

898 _____.
Mountaineering holiday / by Frank S. Smythe. - New
ed. - London: Hodder & Stoughton, 1950. - 248 p. :
plates.

899 _____.
Mountains in colour / by Frank S. Smythe. - Lon-
don: Max Parrish, 1949. - 155 p. : 57 plates.
Also pub. under title, Behold the mountains.

900 _____.
My alpine album / by Frank S. Smythe. - London:
Black, 1940. - 147 p. : 47 plates, map.

901 _____.
Over Tyrolese hills / by Frank S. Smythe. - London: Hodder & Stoughton, 1936. - 276 p. : ill.

902 _____.
The spirit of the hills / by Frank S. Smythe. -
London: Hodder & Stoughton, 1946-1950. - 308 p. :
plates.
First pub. 1935.

903 SMYTHE, Tony
Rock climbers in action in Snowdonia, by T. Smythe.
Ill. by John Cleare, captions / descriptions by Robin G.
Collomb. - London: Secker & Warburg, 1966. - 127
p. : 32 plates, map.

904 SNAITH, Stanley
Alpine adventure / by Stanley Snaith. - London:
Percy Press, 1944. - v. 153 p. : plates.

905 _____.
At grips with Everest / by S. Snaith. - London: Percy
Press, 1944. - v. 153 p. : plates.

"Intended for young readers--this book has short accounts of the attempts to climb Mount Everest plus other mountains in the Himalayas. " BRD.

906 _____.
The mountain challenge/ by Stanley Snaith. - London: Percy Pr. , 1952. - 158 p. : plates.

907 SNYDER, Howard H.
The hall of the mountain king/ by Howard H. Snyder. - 207 p.
"On June 25th, 1967, the twelve members of Wilcox Mount McKinley expedition began their ascent ... only five of them came back down. The story of the climb ... the raging storm and the crucial errors of judgement which led to the deaths of seven men. " Speleobooks.

908 SOMERVELL, Theodore Howard
After Everest: the experiences of a mountaineer and medical missionary/ by T. Howard Somervell. - London: Hodder & Stoughton, 1936. - 339 p. : plates, port.
"Account of two seasons spent in climbing among the Oberland peaks or at Zermatt, two expeditions to Everest in 1922 and 1924, as well as climbs done in Kumaon, on the south side of Kanchenjunga, round Nanda Devi, and at the foot of Nanga Parbat. " Yakushi.
See also REASON, Joyce (983)

909 SOPER, Jack
The Black cliff: history of rock climbing on Clogwyn Du'r Arddu/ by J. Soper, Ken Wilson and Peter Crew. - London: Kaye and Ward, 1971. - 158 p. : ill. , ports. , bibl.

SOPER, N. J. see JONES, Trevor (493)

910 SOUTH AFRICAN RAILWAYS, Publicity Dept.
The Drakensberg National Park: South Africa's mountain playground. - Johannesburg: South African Railways and Harbours Administration, 1937. - 31 p. : ill.

911 _____.
Mountaineering in South Africa/ South African Railways. - Johannesburg: South African Railways, 1914. - 62 p. : ill. , maps.

912 SPECTORSKY, Auguste G.
Book of the mountains: being a collection of writings about the mountains in all of their aspects/ by A. G. Spectorsky. - New York: Appleton-Century-Crofts, 1955. - 492 p. : ill. , plates.
"Unexpectedly broad in scope--general human appeal plus literary merit with over sixty pages of black and white photographs. Invaluable for reference purposes, definitely recommended. " BRD.

913 SPENCER, Sydney
Mountaineering/ by Sydney Spencer. - London: Seeley Service, 1934. - 383 p. : 102 plates, 9 maps, bibl.
"This volume in the Lonsdale Library consists of chapters by Alpine Club experts on the historical and technical aspects of mountaineering, and on the chief climbing ranges of the world. " NBL.

914 SPENDER, Edward Harold
Through the high Pyrenees/ by Edward Spender; with ill. and supplementary sections by H. Llewellyn Smith. - London: Innes, 1898. - 370 p. (Bibliography of Pyrenees)

915 SPINDLER, Robert
Die Alpen in der englischen Literatur und Kunst/ by Dr. Robert Spindler. - Leipzig: Verlag von Bernhard Tauchnity, 1932. - 31 p. : plates.
Facsim. reprint by Johnson Reprint Co. , 1967. Cover title: Beiträge zur englischen Philologie/ hrsg. von Max Forster. A very superficial treatment of the Alps in the English literature and disappointing in its scarcity of references even for 1932. Ed.

SPRING, Ira see SPRING, Robert

SPRING, Norma see SPRING, Robert

SPRING, Patricia see SPRING, Robert

916 SPRING, Robert
Adventuring on Mt. Rainier/ by Bob Spring. - Seattle: Superior Publishing Co.

917 _____ .
High adventure: mountain photography by Bob and

Ira Spring/ text by Norma and Patricia Spring. - Seattle: Superior Publishing Co. , 1951. - 115 p. : ill.

918   .
High worlds of the mountain climber/ mountain photography by Bob and Ira Spring; text by Harvey Manning. - Seattle: Superior Publishing Co. , 1959. - 142 p. : ill. , plates, ports.

STARK, Elizabeth see JACKSON, Monica (481)

919 STEAD, Richard
Adventures on the high mountains: romantic incidents and perils of travel, sport and exploration throughout the world/ by R. Stead. - London: Seeley & Co. , 1908. - 327 p. : 16 ill.

920   .
Great mountaineers/ by R. Stead. - London: Seeley Service. (Daring deeds series)

921 STEBBING, E. P.
Stalks in the Himalaya/ by E. P. Stebbing. - London: Lane, 1912. - 321 p. : ill

922 STEELE, Peter
Doctor on Everest: a personal account of the 1971 expedition/ by Peter Steele; line drawings by Phoebe Bullock. - London: Hodder & Stoughton, 1972. - 222 p. : ill. , maps, plates, 22 cm.
"Personal account of the 1971 International Mount Everest, SW face, led by Norman Dyrenfurth. " Yakushi.

923 STEPHEN, Sir Leslie
Men, books and mountains/ ed. by S. O. A. Ullman. - Minnesota: University Press, 1957. - 247 p. : bibl.
Contains two essays on mountaineering from an address to the Alpine Club. Depicts the notion of climbing with guides and recreates the period very well. Ed.

924   .
The playground of Europe/ by Sir Leslie Stephen. - London: Longmans, 1871.
"Ascents of Zinalrothorn and Schreckhorn; crossings of the Eigerjoch, the Jungfraujoch, the Vierscherjoch. Reflects the social pleasures of climbing ... puts the sport in its historical and literary context. " NBL.

925 _____.
Sunset on Mont Blanc / by Sir Leslie Stephen. -
London: 1873.
See also MAITLAND, Frederic William (585)

926 STEPHENS, I.
Horned moon / by I. Stephens. - London: Chatto &
Windus, 1953.

927 STERN
Mountain panoramas from Pamirs / by Stern. - London: Murray, 1936.

928 STOBERT, Tom
Adventurer's eye: the autobiography of Everest
filmman Tom Stobert / by Tom Stobert. - London: Od-
ham's Press, 1958. - 256 p. : ill.
"The author joined as a cameraman to the Everest
expedition of 1953. " Yakushi.

929 STOCK, E. E.
Scrambles in storm and sunshine among the Swiss
and English Alps / by E. E. Stock. - J. Ouseley, 1911. -
210 p.

930 [no entry]

931 STODDARD, Frederick Wolcott
Tramps through Tyrol / by F. W. Stoddard. - London: Mills & Boon, 1912. - 298 p. : ill.

932 STUCK, Hudson
Ascent of Denali (Mt. McKinley); a narrative of the
first complete ascent of the highest peak in North America / by Hudson Stuck. - New York: Scribner's, 1914. -
xix, 188 p. : ill.
"Clear, vigorous writing by the Archdeacon of Yukon
of a masterly expedition. " RHB.

933 STUTFIELD, Hugh E. M.
Climbs and explorations in the Canadian Rockies /
by Hugh E. M. Stutfield and John Norman Collie. -
London: Longmans, 1903. - xii, 342 p. : ill. , maps.
"The author writes vividly about the semi wilderness.
Great peaks soothed his spirit yet fired his love for the
unexplored. " RHB.

934   STYLES, Frank Showell
       The Arrow book of climbing/ by Showell Styles. -
London: Arrow books, 1967. - 192 p. : ill. , 8 plates,
diagr.
       First pub. under title, The foundations of climbing;
London, S. Paul, 1966.

935   _____.
       Blue remembered hills/ by Showell Styles. - Lon-
don: Faber, 1965. - 189 p. : ill. , map.
       The early biography of the author from his hill-
walking days to the Dolomites, Alps, and Atlas mountains of Algeria.   Professionally written with enthusiasm
and experience. Ed.

936   _____.
       A climber in Wales/ by Showell Styles. - Birming-
ham: Cornish, 1947. - 85 p. : ill.

937   _____.
       The climber's bedside book/ by Showell Styles. -
London: Faber, 1965, 1968. - 256 p. : 4 ill. , bibl.
       Assorted true stories of a mountaineering nature,
biographies of fifty mountaineers, details of a hundred
notable mountains for handy reference. Ed.

938   _____.
       First on the summits/ by Showell Styles; with dia-
grams by R. B. Evans. - London: Gollancz, 1970. -
157 p. : 12 plates, ill. , maps, ports.
       Accounts of the first ascents of the world's 12 ma-
jor peaks. Ed.

939   _____.
       First up Everest/ text by Showell Styles, illus. by R.
Briggs. - London: Hamilton, 1969. (Briggs book)
       For children.

940   _____.
       Foundations of climbing/ by Showell Styles. - Lon-
don: Stanley Paul, 1966. - 144 p. : 24 plates, ill. ,
diagrs.
       With forty years' experience behind him, the author
has written a book for beginners that for all its attempts reflects outdated attitudes and techniques. Ed.

941   _____.
       Getting to know mountains/ by Showell Styles; ed.

by Jack Cox. - London: Newnes, 1958. - 160 p. : 6
plates, bibl.

942   .

        How mountains are climbed/ by Showell Styles. -
London: Routledge & Kegan Paul, 1958. - 158 p. : 8
plates, bibl. (How series/ ed. by Phoebe Snow)

943   .

        An introduction to mountaineering/ by Showell
Styles. - 1955. - London: Seeby Service, 1954. - 159
p. : 7 plates, bibl. (Beaufort Library, ed. by Duke of
Beaufort, vol. 4)

944   .

        Mallory of Everest/ by Showell Styles. - London:
Hamish Hamilton, 1967. - 157 p. : 12 plates (incl.
ports), maps, diagrs.

945   .

        Men and mountaineering: an anthology of writings
by climbers/ ed. by Showell Styles. - London: Hamilton, 1968. - 207 p. : (Hamish Hamilton collections)
        Twenty-three selections in chronological order from
Wills on the Wetterhorn in 1854 to Robbins on El Capi-
tan in 1964. It is unfortunately lacking in illustration. Ed.

946   .

        The moated mountain/ by Showell Styles. - London:
Hurst & Blackett, 1955. - 255 p. : col. front, plates
(incl. ports), map.
        "... He wrote the tale of his own Himalayan expe-
dition to Baudha Peak, the Moated Mountain, in the Manaslu group in 1954 by the four members and the four
Sherpas. Unfortunately, it ended as only reconnaissance. " Yakushi.

947   .

        Modern mountaineering/ by F. S. Styles, with a
foreword by John Jackson. - London: Faber & Faber,
1964. - 189 p. : ill. , 8 plates, diagrs. , bibl. , 21 1/2 cm.
        "... Combines an account of the basic craft of
mountaineering from simple hill walking to advanced
climbing on rock and ice, and even includes instruction
in the use of mechanical aids. " John Morris, in the
Listener.

948

‾‾‾‾‾‾ Mountaineers' weekend book/ by Showell Styles, de-
corated by Thomas Beck. - London: Seeley Service,
1951. - 407 p.
A compendium of all aspects of mountaineering. Ed.

949

‾‾‾‾‾‾ Mountains of the midnight sun: an account of the
British Lyngen expedition 1952/ by Showell Styles. -
London: Hurst & Blackett, 1954. - 208 p. : 14 plates,
ports.

950

‾‾‾‾‾‾ On top of the world: an illustrated history of mountaineering and mountaineers/ by Showell Styles; with an
intro. by Fosco Maraini. - London: Hamish Hamilton,
1967. - 278 p. : 158 p. : 158 ill. , plates, maps, 25 1/2 cm.
The author has not progressed beyond the state of
climbing in 1945--the stories have all been told before;
technical climbing is handled poorly and modern exploits
not understood. Ed.

951

‾‾‾‾‾‾ Rock and rope/ by Showell Styles. - London: Faber
& Faber, 1967. - 174 p. : 8 plates.
The "apologia of a middle-aged climber ... with a
fine record, including a Himalayan expedition. But he
has specialised in the opening up of outlaying crags and
the pioneering of routes in the Moderate to Very Difficult class which he names with a pretty turn of wit. "
Times Literary Supplement.

952

‾‾‾‾‾‾ Walks and climbs in Malta/ by Showell Styles. -
Valetta: Progressive Press, 1944. - 79 p.

STYRSA, Josef see HECKEL, Vilem (422)

953 SUMMERS, Clinton Long Macdonald
Adventure activities in physical education/ by C. L.
M. Summers. - London: Blackwell, 1963. - 85 p. : 4
plates, diagrs. , bibl. (Books for teachers)

954 SUTTON, Geoffrey
Artificial aids to mountain climbing/ by Geoffrey
Sutton. - London: Kaye & Ward, under the auspices
of the Mountaineering Association, 1962. - 64 p. : ill. ,
diagrs. , 18 1/2 cm.

955 _____ .
Samson: the life and writings of Menlove Edwards;
with biographical memoir / by Geoffrey Sutton and Wilfred Noyce. - n. p. : privately printed, 1960. - 122 p. : ill.
See also BYNE, Eric (155); YOUNG, Geoffrey Winthrop (1131)

956 SWISS ALPINE CLUB
Mountaineering handbook: a complete and practical
guide for beginner or expert / London: Paternoster
Press, for the Association of British Members of the
Swiss Alpine Club, 1950. - 163 p. : ill.

957 SWISS FOUNDATION FOR MOUNTAIN RESEARCH
Everest: the Swiss Expedition in photographs. -
London: Hodder & Stoughton, 1954. - 150 plates, map.
"Picture book of the Swiss expeditions to Everest
in spring and autumn of 1952. " Yakushi.

958 SWISS NATIONAL TOURIST OFFICE
Mountaineering in Switzerland. - Zurich: Swiss National Tourist Office, 1950's. - 43 p. : ill.

959 SYDNEY ROCKCLIMBING CLUB
The rock climbs of New South Wales / comp. by
members of the S. R. C. - Sydney, N. S. W. ; the club,
1963. - 112 p. : ill. , maps.

960 SYKES, Sir Percy
A history of exploration / by Sir Percy Sykes. -
2nd ed. - New York: 1936. - 274 p. : 25 ill. , 35 maps.
"Includes a section on modern explorers in Tibet. "
Dawson's.

961 SYMINGTON, Noel Howard
The nightclimbers of Cambridge / by Whipplesnaith
(pseud.). - 2nd ed. - London: Chatto & Windus, 1952. -
First pub. 1952. - 183 p. : plates, ports.
"A curious classic. Illegal and highly unorthodox
climbs, subject to the hazards of proctors below as well
as crumbling architecture above. Brilliant flashlight
pictures. " NBL.

962 SYNGE, Patrick M.
Mountains of the moon: an expedition to the equatorial mountains of Africa / by Patrick M. Synge. - London: Lindsay Drummond, 1937. - xxiv, 221 p. : plates,
maps.

TAIRRAZ, Pierre see FRISON-ROCHE, Roger (350); REBUFFET, Gaston (784)

963 TALBOT, Daniel
Treasury of mountaineering stories/ by Daniel Talbot. - London: Davies, 1955. - 282 p.

964 TALFOURD, Thomas Noon
Vacation rambles and thoughts/ by T. N. Talfourd. - Moxon, 1845. - 2v.
Contents: v. 1. A first visit to the Alps 1841. The Alps revisited, 1842. v. 2. Chamouni revisited.

TARAUA TRAMPING CLUB see BRIDGE, L. D. (113)

964a TARBURCK, Kenneth
Nylon rope and climbing safety/ by K. Tarbuck. - Edinburgh: British Ropes, 19[00's]. - 35 p.: ill.

965 TAYLOR, Peter
Coopers Creek to Lang Tang II/ by Peter Taylor. - Adelaide, Rigby, 1964. - 239 p.: ill., plates.
"Account of the author's expedition to Lang Tang II, 21,592 ft., in 1964." Yakushi.

TAYLOR, Richard see NOYCE, Wilfred Cuthbert Francis (706)

965a TEMPLE, Philip
Castles in the air; men and mountains in New Zealand/ ed. by Philip Temple. - Dunedin, New Zealand: John McIndoe, 1973. - 168 p.: ill., chiefly plates.
An amazing book of photographs and paintings of New Zealand mountaineering, including a history of the sport in that country. Ed.

966 _____.
The sea and the snow: Heard Island expedition/ by P. Temple. - London: Cassell, 1967.

967 _____.
The world at their feet: the story of New Zealand mountaineers in the great ranges of the world/ by Philip Temple. - Christchurch, Whitcombe & Tombs, 1969. - 256 p.: ill., maps, ports.

968 TENZING Norgay
Man of Everest: the autobiography of Tenzing/

Told to James Ramsey Ullman. - London: Harrap,
1955. - 320 p. : col. front. , ill. , 35 plates (incl. 3 col.)
    Also pub. , London: Transworld Press, 1957 (Corgi
books, no. G419). "Experiences on many expeditions in
the last 20 years culminating in the ascent of Everest. "
NBL.

969   .
        Tiger of the snows: the autobiography of Tenzing
of Everest/ by Tenzing in collaboration with James
Ramsey Ullman. - New York: Putnam, 1955.
    Also published under titles, Man of Everest, and
Tenzing: Tiger of Everest. "One of the best books on
Everest from a verbal account of the life and impres-
sions of a native of the region. Vivid insight into the
Oriental mind. " BRD.
    See also MALARTIC, Yves (586); CHARLES, Wynd-
ham (171)

970 TERRAY, Lionel
        Borders of the impossible: from the Alps to An-
napurna/ by Lionel Terray, trans. from the French by
Geoffrey Sutton. - New York: Doubleday, 1964. - 350
p. : ill. , maps.
    "The author's autobiography of mountain climbing,
from the Alps to the Himalaya, including the French
Annapurna expedition of 1950 led by M. Herzog, the
French Makula and Janna expeditions. He was killed
by a fall from a rock slab at training in 1965. " Yakushi.

971   .
        Conquistadores of the useless: from the Alps to
Annapurna/ by L. Terray. - trans. from the French by
Geoffrey Sutton. - London: Gollancz, 1963. - 351 p. :
plates (incl. ports.), maps.
    Orig. pub. as Les Conquerants de l'inutile; Paris:
Gallimard, 1961.
    See also FRANCO, Jean (335)

972 THOMAS, Lowell
        Lowell Thomas' book of the high mountains/ by Lo-
well Thomas. - London: Simon & Schuster, 1964.
    "Unique in the mountain literature of the world. "
William O. Douglas.

973 THOMPSON, Arthur J.
        Ortler Alps: Ortles, Zebru, Trafoir Wall, Cevedal:
a selection of popular and recommended climbs/ by Ar-

thur J. Thompson. - Reading, Berks. : West Col Productions, 1968. - 98 p. : ill. , maps.
See also THORINGTON, James Monroe (979)

974 THOMPSON, Dorothy Evelyn
Climbing with Joseph Georges/ by Dorothy Evelyn
Thompson. - Kendal, Westmd. : Wilson, 1962. - 159 p. :
12 plates.
"An Alpine guide. "

975 THOMSON, J. M. Archer
Climbing in the Ogwen district/ by J. M. A. Thomson. - London: Edward Arnold, for the Climbers' Club,
1910. - xx, 154 p.

976 _____ .
The climbs on Lliwedd/ by J. M. A. Thomson and
A. W. Andrews. - London: Edward Arnold, for the
Climbers' Club, 1909. - xv, 99 p. : 20 ill. , 8 diagrs.

977 THOMSON, Joseph
Travels in the Atlas and southern Morocco: a narrative of exploration/ by Joseph Thomson. - London:
Philip, 1889. - 488 p. : ill. , maps.
"Contents: Ascent of the iron mountain. - Camp at
Jebel Hadid. - Views of the Atlas mountains. - Ascent
of Iraghalsor. - Ascent of Gadal. - Descriptions of
mountain scenery. - Evidences of glacial action. - Ascent of Yaurirf. " Campbell, J. I. (157)

978 THORINGTON, James Munroe
Climber's guide to the interior ranges of British
Columbia/ by J. M. Thorington. - 2nd ed. - New York:
American Alpine Club, 1947. - 152 p. : 5 plates, front,
ill. , maps, bibl.

979 _____ .
A climber's guide to the Rocky Mountains of Canada/
by J. M. Thorington. - 6th ed. - with the collab. of
Arthur J. Thompson. - New York: American Alpine
Club, 1966. - 377 p. : maps.

980 _____ .
The glittering mountains of Canada/ by J. M. Thorington. - Philadelphia: 1925.

981 _____ .
The Lyell and Freshfield glaciers, Canadian Rocky

Mountains, 1926 etc. / by J. Monroe Thorington. -
Washington, D. C. : Smithsonian Institution, 1927. - 8 p. :
12 plates. (Smithsonian miscellaneous collections, vol.
78, no. 6)

982 _____ .
Mont Blanc sideshow: the life and times of Albert
Smith/ by J. M. Thorington. - Philadelphia: J. C.
Winston, 1934. - 255 p. : plates, ports.
"Exposes Smith as a vulgarizer of the mountains;
describes the lectures at Egyptian Hall where St. Ber-
nard dogs distributed chocolates!" RHB.

983 _____ .
A survey of early American ascents in the Alps in
the nineteenth century/ by J. M. Thorington. - New
York: American Alpine Club, 1943. - 83 p. : front, ill.,
bibl.
See also KAIN, Conroad (494); PALMER, Howard
S. (731)

984 THWAITES, Reuben Gold
A brief history of Rocky Mountain exploration: with
special reference to the expedition of Lewis and Clark/
Reuben Gold Thwaites. - New York: 1904. - 276 p. : ill.

985 TICHY, Herbert
Cho Oyu, by favour of the gods/ by Herbert Tichy,
trans. from the German by Basil Creighton. - London:
Methuon, 1957. - 196 p. : 35 plates, maps, 21 1/2 cm.

986 _____ .
Himalaya/ by Herbert Tichy; trans. by Richard
Rickett and David Streatfield. - New York: Putnam,
1971. - 174 p. : ill., plates, map.
History, geography and ethnology together with
climbing experiences that include the first ascent of Cho
Oyu. Sherpas and the Abominable Snowman. Ed.

987 TILMAN, Harold William
Ascent of Nanda Devi/ by Harold Tilman, with a
foreword by T. G. Longstaff. - Cambridge: University
Press, 1927. - 235 p. : plates, map, 21 cm.
"The successful climb by a small Anglo-American
party two years after the Shipton-Tilman expedition. " NBL.

988 _____ .
China to Chitral/ by Harold Tilman. - Cambridge:

University Press, 1951. - 123 p. : 69 plates.
"A traveller's book written by a witty essayist and
tale teller. The actual voyage across China. " BRD.

989 _____ .
Mischief in Greenland/ by Harold Tilman. - Cambridge: University Press, 1950's.

990 _____ .
Mischief in Patagonia/ by Harold Tilman. - Cambridge: University Press, 1957. - 185 p. : ill. , 8
plates, maps, 21 cm.

991 _____ .
Mount Everest: 1938/ by Harold Tilman. - Cambridge: University Press, 1948. - 159 p. : maps, 33
plates.
"A straightforward account of two unsuccessful attempts on Everest in 1938 written in the author's char-
acteristic dry humour. " BRD.

992 _____ .
Nepal Himalaya/ by H. W. Tilman. - Cambridge:
University Press, 1952. - 271 p. : 61 plates.
"Journeys in 1949 and 1950 in Langlang Himal and
Annapurna Himal, the first visit to the south side of
Everest. " NBL.   "Subdued tones of dry humour and
ripe philosophy of an Englishman. " BRD.

993 _____ .
Snow on the equator/ by Harold William Tilman. -
London: Bell, 1937. - 265 p. : maps, plates.
"Among details of life as planter there are accounts
of the author's feats of mountain climbing. The author
makes mountain climbing sound like a nice sensible
pastime for anyone--an illusion the accompanying photographs promptly dispel. " BRD.

994 _____ .
Two mountains and a river/ by H. W. Tilman. -
Cambridge: University Press, 1949. - 232 p. : 36 plates.
"An attempt on Rakapashi, a journey across the
Karakoram to join Shipton at Kasgar, back to Pakistan
by the Oxus. " NBL.

995 _____ .
When men and mountains meet/ by Harold Tilman.-

Cambridge: University Press. - 232 p. : maps, 54
plates, 21 1/2 cm.
"A record of strictly personal adventure, two-thirds
about the author's experiences during the war but not
away from high places and high adventure. " BRD.

TIRICH MIR, Members of the expedition see NORWE-
    GIAN HIMALAYAN EXPEDITION (701)

996   TISSOT, R.
        Mont Blanc / by R. Tissot. - 1924. - ill. , maps.
      (Picture guides)

997   TOLL, Roger W.
        Mountaineering in the Rocky Mountain National Park /
      by Roger W. Toll, comp. from the records of the Colo-
      rado Mountain Club. Ed. by R. S. Yard. - Washington,
      D. C. : U. S. Gov. Printing Office, 1921. - 106 p. : 25
      plates.

998   TOMBAZI, N. A.
        Account of a photographic expedition to the southern
      glaciers of Kanchenjunga in the Sikkim Himalaya / by N.
      A. Tombazi. - Bombay: privately printed, 1925.

999   TRAMPS ROUND THE MOUNTAINS OF THE MOON and
      through the back gate of the Congo / London: Allen &
      Unwin, 1908. - 316 p. : ill. , maps.

1000 TRANTER, Philip
        No tigers in the Hindu Kush / ed. by Nigel Tranter. -
      London: Hodder & Stoughton, 1968. - 155 p. : 17 plates,
      ill. , maps, 21 1/2 cm. (Travel Book Club, 1069)
        A day-to-day diary, edited by his father. The book
      describes a "shoestring" expedition which climbed three
      peaks over 20,000 feet and seven over 10,000, and map-
      ped 50 square miles of previously untrodden region in
      two months. Remarkable. Ed.

      TREMAIN, Jill see DINGLE, Graeme (257)

1001 TRENKER, Luis
        Brothers of the snow / by Luis Trenker, trans. by
      F. H. Lyon. - London: Dutton, 1934. - 247 p. : ill.
        "A famous mountain climber and film producer des-
      cribes his adventures as a Dolomite guide and on the al-
      pine front during the war, the making of two films plus

his later experiences in Hollywood. " BRD.

1002   TRISTRAM, Henry Baker
     Rambles in Japan/ by H. B. Tristram, with illus.
by Edward Whymper. - London: Religious Tract Society, 1895. - 304 p.

TROTT, Otto T. see MARINER, Wastl (592)

1003   TRUFFAUT, Roland
     From Kenya to Kilimanjaro/ by Roland Truffat;
trans. from the French. - London: Hale, 1957. -
155 p. : 24 plates, front. ill. , bibl.
     Orig. pub. as Du Kenya au Kilimanjaro; Paris:
Fulliard, 1953.

1004   TUCKER, John
     Kanchenjunga/ by John Tucker; foreword by Sir
John Hunt. - London: Elek Books, 1955. - 224 p. :
plates, maps, 22 cm.

1005   TUCKETT, Elizabeth
     Zigzagging among Dolomites/ by Elizabeth Tuckett. -
London: Longmans, 1871. - 38 p. : ill.

TUCKETT, Francis Fox see HOWARD, Eliot (455)

1006   TURNER, Samuel
     The conquest of the New Zealand Alps/ by S.
Turner. - London: Fisher Unwin, 1922. - 291 p.
     "A self-centred climber who praised his exploits
in his books but wrote with very modest proficiency. "
RHB.

1007   _____.
     My climbing adventures on four continents/ by
Samuel Turner. - London: Fisher Unwin, 1911. -
283 p. : 74 ill.
     "Reputedly sold well in his day, unlikely to be of
interest today. " RHB.

1008   _____.
     Siberia: a record of travel, climbing and explora-
tion/ by Samuel Turner, with an intro. by Baron Iley-
king. - London: Fisher Unwin, 1905. - 420 p. : 2
maps, plates, 23 cm.

1009   TUTT, J. W.
        Rambles in Alpine valleys / by J. W. Tutt. -
        1899. - ill.

1010   TUTTON, Alfred Edwin Howard
        The natural history of ice and snow: illus. from
        the Alps / by A. E. H. Tutton. - London: Routledge
        and Kegan Paul, 1931. - xvi, 319 p. : 48 pl.

1011   TWITTERS, Peter
        How I went up the Jungfrau, and came down again /
        by Peter Twitters.

1012   TYLER, John Ecclesfield
        The Alpine passes: the Middle Ages, 962-1250 /
        by J. E. Tyler. - Oxford: Basil Blackwell, 1930. -
        188 p.

1013   TYNDALE, Henry Edmund Guise
        Blackwell's mountaineering library / ed. by H. E.
        Tyndale. - Oxford: Blackwell, 1936- .
        Title of a series of books published by Blackwell's.
        Ed.

1014   ───────.
        Mountain paths / by H. E. Tyndale. - London:
        Eyre and Spottiswode, 1948. - 208 p. : plates. (New
        Alpine Library)
        See also KLUCKER, Christian (504)

1015   TYNDALL, John
        The glaciers of the Alps: being a narrative of
        excursions and ascents. An account of the origin and
        phenomena of glaciers, and an exposition of the physi-
        cal principles to which they are related / by John Tyn-
        dall. - London: 1860. - 445 p.
        "Somewhat disconnected in format as a journal,
        but shows throughout the love of mountains and moun-
        taineering. " RHB.

1016   ───────.
        Hours of exercise in the Alps: notes and com-
        ments on ice and glaciers and other scraps; voyage to
        Algeria to observe the eclipse / by John Tyndall. -
        6th ed. - London: Longmans, Green, 1936.
        First pub. 1871. "Famous in his day and still of

interest with accounts of his continuous climbing career
from 1856-1870. " RHB.

1017   .
Mountaineering in 1861: a vacation tour/ by John
Tyndall. - London: Longmans, 1862. - vi, 105 p.
"Tyndall first visited the Alps to study glaciers:
he became one of the most enterprising mountaineers.
He describes his attempts on the Matterhorn; his pi-
oneering ascent of the Weisshorn and numerous other
expeditions. " NBL.
See also EVE, Arthur Stewart (301)

1018 ULLMAN, James Ramsey
Age of mountaineering: with a chapter on British
mountains/ by W. H. Murray. - London: Collins,
1954. - 384 p. : 24 plates, maps, bibl. , 21 cm.
"Based on High Conquest (1941) [1020] this book
continues through the post-war years to Everest.
Written with the excitement of a novel. " BRD.

1019   .
Americans on Everest: the official account of the
ascent led by Norman G. Dyrenfurth/ by J. R. Ullman
and other members of the expedition. - London: Lippincott, 1964. - 429 p. : ill. , 54 plates, maps, 21 1/2 cm.

1020   .
High conquest/ by Ramsey Ullman. - Philadelphia:
Lippincott, 1941. - 334 p. : ill. , maps.
"Told for the beginner, with a wide, interesting
scope in time and place; well illustrated with photo-
graphs. " BRD. See 1018.

1021   .
Kingdom of adventure: Everest, a chronicle of
man's assault on the earth's highest mountain/ narrat-
ed by the participants, with an accompanying text by
J. R. Ullman. - London: Collins, 1948. - 320 p. :
plates.
"Contains extracts by Bruce, Mallory, Norton,
Odell, Scott and Younghusband. One of the most enjoyable books on Everest yet written. " BRD.

1022   .
The other side of the mountain: an escape to the
Amazon/ by J. R. Ullman. - London: Gollancz,
1938. - 382 p.

1023
_____ .
The sands of Karakorum, etc. / by J. R. Ullman. -
London: Collins, 1953. - 256 p.

1024
_____ .
Straight up: the life and death of John Harlin / by
James Ullman. - New York: Doubleday, 1968. - 288
p. : plates.
A controversial biography written as a thriller,
and failing to do justice to the man or his achieve-
ments. Ed.

1025 UMLAUFT, Friedrich
The Alps / by F. Umlauft; trans. from the German
by Louisia Brough. - London: Kegan Paul, 1888. -
523 p. : ill.

1026 UNDERHILL, Miriam
Give me the hills / by Miriam Underhill. - London: Methuen, 1956. - 252 p. : 32 plates.
"A climbing autobiography. [The author] led the
first all-female team up the Monch from the Jungfrau,
traversed the Grepon and climbed the Matterhorn. "
Epolenbooks.

1027 UNDRELL, J.
An account of an ascent to the summit of Mont
Blanc / by J. Undrell. - London: 1821.

1028 U.S. Dept. of the Army.
Mountain operations. - Washington, D.C. : Dept.
of the Army, 1959. - 238 p. : ill. , diagrs.

1029 UNIVERSITY OF NEW ENGLAND [Australia] MOUN-
TAINEERING CLUB
New England tablelands: walking, caving (and)
climbing. - 3rd ed. Armidale, N.S.W. : the club,
1971. - 76 p. : ill. , maps.
A general description of this premier climbing
area of Australia including guides to rock climbs with
illustrations of the Warrumbungles. Ed.

1030 UNSWORTH, Walter
Because it's there / by Walter Unsworth. - London:
Gollancz, 1968. - 144 p. : 8 plates.
Short biographies of famous mountaineers, 1840-
1940. Ed.

1031

_____ .
The book of rock climbing/ by Walter Unsworth. - London: Barker, 1968. - 112 p. : ill. , bibl. , index.

1032

_____ .
The English outcrops/ by Walter Unsworth; with a foreword by Jack Langland. - London: Gollancz, 1964. - 192 p. : ill. , 16 plates, maps, tables, diagrs. , bibl.

1033

_____ .
Matterhorn man: the life and adventures of Edward Whymper/ by Walter Unsworth. - London: Gollancz, 1965. - 127 p. : ill. , 8 plates, 4 maps, bibl.

1034

_____ .
North face: the second conquest of the Alps/ by W. Unsworth, with a foreword and photographs by Chris Bonnington. - London: Hutchinson, 1969. - 160 p. : 12 plates, ill. , maps, 19 1/2 cm. (Men in action)
A book of the greatest Alpine climbs; those on the north faces of the Brenva, Mont Blanc, Dru, Cima Grande, Eiger: an honor role of technical climbing. Ed.

1035

_____ .
Tiger of the snows: the life and adventures of A. F. Mummery/ by Walter Unsworth. - London: Gollancz, 1967. - 126 p. : 8 plates (incl. ports.) maps, diagr. , bibl.

1036

_____ .
The young mountaineer/ by Walter Unsworth. - London: Hutchinson, 1959. - 191 p.

UNTERHILL, Miriam see UNDERHILL, Miriam (1026)

1037 VAN DYKE, John Charles
The mountain: renewed studies in impressions and appearances/ by J. C. Van Dyke. - London: Werner Laurie, 1916. - xvi, 234 p.

VAUCHER, Michel see ZERMATTEN, Maurice (1139)

VENEMA, G. see BRONERSMA, Leo Daniel (121)

1038 VERGHESE, B. G.
Himalayan endeavour/ by B. G. Verghese. - Bom-

bay: Bennett Coleman, 1962. - 155 p. : plates, maps, 21 1/2 cm.

1039 VISSER-HOOFT, Jenny
Among the Karakoram Glaciers in 1925/ by J. Visser-Hooft; with contrib. by Ph. C. Visser. - London: Edward Arnold, 1925. - 303 p. : ill.

1040 VOGE, Harvey H.
A climber's guide to the High Sierra: routes and records for California peaks from Bond Pass to Army Pass, and for rock climbs in Yosemite Valley and King Canyon/ ed. by Harvey Voge. - San Francisco: Sierra Club, 1954. - 301 p. : ill. , bibl.

1041 _____ .
The mountaineer's guide to the High Sierra/ ed. by H. H. Voge and A. J. Smatko. - San Francisco: Sierra Club, 1973.

1042 WAINWRIGHT, A.
The fell walker/ by A. Wainwright. - Westmoreland Gazette, 1966.
The story behind the hill walking guide books. Ed.

1043 WALKER, J. Hubert
Mountain days in the highlands and Alps/ by J. Hubert Walker. - London: Edward Arnold, 1937. - 320 p. : ill.

1044 WALL, David
Rondoy, an expedition to the Peruvian Andes/ by David Wall, with a foreword by Don Whillans. - London: Murray, 1965. - 176 p. : 26 plates, maps, 21 1/2 cm.

1045 WALLER, James
The everlasting hills: an account of the 1938 attempt on Masherbrum, in the Karakorum/ by J. Waller. - Edinburgh and London: Blackwood & Sons, 1939. - xii, 190 p. : 64 ill.
Climbing progress of a yound subaltern in the Himalayas. Ed. "Record of the expedition to Masherbrum in 1938, organized by the author, including the small expeditions to NUN and to Peak 36 (Saltoro Kangri) of 1935. " Yakushi.

1046   WALTON, William Howard Murray
        Scrambles in Japan and Formosa/ by W. H. M.
        Walton. - London: Edward Arnold, 1934. - 304 p. :
        25 plates, 2 maps.
        "Expeditions all over the Japanese Alps between
        1917 and 1932. " NBL. "Descriptions of tours and
        climbing expeditions on good and bad rock, ascents,
        escarpments ... with a description of the famous
        East Coast Cliff which drops down to the sea from
        8,000 feet. " BRD.

1047   WARD, Alexander
        Climbing and mountain walking in Mauritius: par-
        ticularly for those who would like to know the Mauri-
        tius Mountain but who do not know the way/ by Alex-
        ander Ward. - Port Louis, Mauritius: P. Mackay,
        196?. - 28 p. : ill. , maps.

1048   WARD, Michael
        In this short span: a mountaineering memoir/ by
        Michael Ward. - London: Victor Gollancz, 1972. -
        304 p. : ill. , 5 maps, plates, 22 1/2 cm.
        "Himalayan mountaineering and exploration. "
        Dawson's.

1049   _____ .
        The mountaineer's companion. (Symposium)/ by
        Michael Ward. - London: Eyre and Spottiswoode,
        1966. - 600 p. : 43 ill.
        A well-illustrated anthology of writings on moun-
        taineering, focusing on the ascent of Mt. Everest, of
        which the author was part of the successful 1953 ex-
        pedition. Ed.

1050   WARWICK, Alan R.
        With Whymper in the Alps/ by A. R. Warwick. -
        London: Muller, (n. d.). - 143 p. : 12 plates, 18 ill. ,
        index, bibl.

1051   WASHBURN, Bradford
        Among the Alps with Bradford/ by Bradford Wash-
        burn.

1052   _____ .
        Bradford on Mount Fairweather/ by Bradford Wash-
        burn. - New York: Putnam, 1931. - 127 p. : ill.
        "The detailed record of an attempt to climb Mount

Fairweather, the highest peak in the Alaskan coastal range: hasty but lively reading. " BRD.
See also HORIZON, New York (449)

WATSON, A. see ALEXANDER, Sir Henry (17)

1053 WATSON, Sir Norman
Round mystery mountain (Mount Waddington): a ski adventure / by Sir Norman Watson. - London: Edward Arnold, 246 p. : ill.

1054 WEDDERBURN, Ernest Alexander Maclagan
Alpine climbing on foot and ski / by E. A. M. Wedderburn. - 2nd rev. ed. rev. by C. Douglas Milner. - London: Country goer, 1954. - 131 p. : 8 plates. First pub. 1937.

1055 ─────.
The technique of alpine mountaineering / by E. A. M. Wedderburn. - 1935.

1056 WEGNER, A.
Mountaineering / by A. Wegner. - London: Lonsdale.

1057 WEIR, Thomas
Camps and climbs in Arctic Norway / by Thomas Weir. - London: Cassell, 1953. - 85 p. : plates.

1058 ─────.
East of Katmandu: on the author's experiences mountaineering in Nepal / by Thomas Weir. - Edinburgh: Oliver & Boyd, 1955. - 138 p. : plates, maps, 21 1/2 cm.
"Account of a mountaineering trip to Nepal; overshadowed by material on the villages, plants and human nature. " BRD.

1059 ─────.
Focus on mountains / by Thomas Weir, ill. by Joan Tebbut. - Edinburgh: McDougalls, 1065. - 80 p. : ill. , bibl.

1060 ─────.
Highland days / Tom Weir. - London: Cassell, 1948. - 139 p. : maps, 35 plates.
A personal account of experiences in British hills-- the photographs are more of scenery than actual climbing. Ed.

1061 _____.
The ultimate mountains: an account of four months'
mountain exploring in the central Himalaya/ by Tom
Weir. - London: Cassell, 1953. - 98 p. : plates.

1062 WEST, Lionel F.
The climber's pocket book: rock climbing acci-
dents, with ... methods of rescue/ by Lionel F.
West. - Manchester: Scientific Pub. , 1907. - 76 p. : ill.

1063 WESTMORELAND, Rusty H.
Adventures in climbing/ by Rusty Westmoreland. -
London: Pelham, 1964. - 124 p. : 8 plates. (Adventurers'
Library)
"Tales of personal experience by a Lakes District
climber taught by George Abraham interwoven with ad-
vice to youngsters interested in climbing. " BBN.

1064 WESTON, Walter
Mountaineering and exploration in the Japanese
Alps/ by the Rev. Walter Weston, foreword by Shige-
taka-Juko-Shiga. - London: Murray, 1896. - 346 p. :
35 ill. , maps, 21 cm.

1065 _____.
The playground of the Far East/ by Rev. Walter
Weston. - London: Murray, 1918. - 333 p. : maps,
ill. , Japan.

1066 WEXLER, Arnold
Theory of belaying/ by Arnold Wexler.

1067 WHEELOCK, Walt
Climbing Mt. Whitney/ by Walt Wheelock and Tom
Condon. Illus. by Ruth Daly. - Glendale, Calif. : La
Siesta, 1960. - 36 p. : ill. , maps.

1068 _____.
Ropes, knots and sling for climbers/ by Walt
Wheelock; illus. by Ruth Daly. - Glendale, Calif. : La-
Siesta, 1960. - 35 p. : ill. , tables.

1069 WHERRY, George Edward
Alpine notes and the climbing foot/ by George E.
Wherry. - Cambridge: Macmillan & Baues, 1896. -
xvi, 174 p. : ill.
"Mr. Wherry was a surgeon as well as a mountain

climber and the second half of his book is devoted to exercises and instructions for developing a good climbing foot.   There are some fascinating illustrations to accompany the instructions. " Dawson's.

1070   _____ .
        Notes from a knapsack/ by George E. Wherry. - Cambridge: Baues & Burns, 1909. - viii, 312 p. : ill.

1071 WHILLANS, Don
        Don Whillans: portrait of a mountaineer/ by D. Whillans and Alick Ormerod. - London: Heineman, 1971. - 266 p. : 16 plates, ill. , 22 1/2 cm.
        Biography of a "tiger" includes rock climbs in England, the Alps, Himalayas and Yosemite. Interesting personal narrative based on a series of diaries. Ed.

        WHIPPLESNAITH (pseud.) see SYMINGTON, Noel Howard (961)

1072 WHITE, Anne Terry
        All about mountains and mountaineering/ by Anne Terry White. - New York: Random, 1961. - 144 p. : ill. (Allabout Books)

1073 WHITE, Walter
        To Mont Blanc and back again/ by Walter White. London: Routledge, 1854. - 208 p.

1074 WHITEHEAD, John
        Exploration of Mount Kina Balu, North Borneo/ by J. Whitehead. - London: Gurney & Jackson, 1893. - x, 317 p. : col. plates.

1075 WHYMPER, Edward
        The ascent of the Matterhorn/ by Edward Whymper. - London: Murray, 1879. - 325 p. : maps, ill.

1076   _____ .
        Chamonix and the range of Mont Blanc: a guide ... with illustrations and maps/ by Edward Whymper. - London: John Murray, 1896. - xiv, 189 p.

1077   _____ .
        A letter addressed to the members of the Alpine Club/ by Edward Whymper. - London: Alpine Club, 1900.

1078 _____.
Man on the Matterhorn/ ed. by M. Dodderidge. -
London: Murray, 1940. - 134 p. : (Journeys and ad-
ventures)
Edited from the author's Scrambles among the
Alps (1079). Ed.

1079 _____.
Scrambles among the Alps, in the years 1860-
1869/ by Edward Whymper. - 4th ed. - London: Murray, 1871. - 468 p. : 8 ill. , plates, 22 cm.
The record of an amazing five years climbing Ec-
rins, Aiguille d'Argentière, Trelatele, Mont Dolent,
Grandes Jorasses, and Aiguille Verte culminating in
1865 with the death of four climbers on the descent. Ed.

1080 _____.
Travels among the Great Andes of the equator/
by Edward Whymper. - London: Murray, 1892. -
456 p. : maps, ill. 2nd ed/ by F. S. Smythe. - London: Lehman, 1949. - 272 p. (Chiltern Library, no.
28)
"Whymper visited the Andes of Equador in 1879
with his old guide and Matterhorn rival, Carrel. Ascents of Chimborazo, Cotopaxi, Cayambe. " NBL.

1081 _____.
The valley of Zermatt and the Matterhorn: a guide
with illustrations and maps/ by Edward Whymper. -
London: John Murray, 1897.
See also GOS, Charles 369a; SMYTHE, Frank Syd-
ney (892); UNSWORTH, Walter (1033); WARWICK, Alan
R. (1050); YOUNG, Bert Edward (1123).

1082 WIBBERLEY, Leonard
The epics of Everest/ by Leonard Wibberley; ill.
by Genevieve Vaughan-Jackson. - London: Faber,
1955. - 217 p. : ill. , maps, plates.
"A history of Everest from the discovery by the
British in 1849 to Hillary and Tenzing's success in the
form of a graphic description of human effort and
courage. " BRD.

WICKS, J. H. see DENT, Clinton Thomas (251)

1083 WIGNALL, Sydney
Prisoner in Red Tibet/ by the leader of the Welsh

Himalayan Expedition, 1955. - London: Hutchinson,
1957. - 264 p. : 33 ill. , map.
"Account of the Welsh expedition to the Saipal
range of NW-Nepal in 1955. For bad weather they
decided to withdraw at the foot of Saipall.... But they
were taken to Taklakot by Chinese troops and held for
two months as spies. " Yakushi.

1084 WILBRAHAM, Edward B.
Narrative of an ascent of Mont Blanc; in August,
1830/ by Edward B. Wilbraham.

1085 WILCOX, Walter Dwight
Camping in the Canadian Rockies: with a sketch
of the early explorations/ by W. D. Wilcox. - New
York: Putnam, 1896. - 283 p. : ill.

1086 _____.
Rockies of Canada/ by W. D. Wilcox.
"Fine pictures of the early days of Canadian moun-
taineering. " RHB.

1087 WILKERSON, James A.
Medicine for mountaineering: handbook for treatment of accidents and illness in remote areas/ by
Doctor James A. Wilkinson. - Seattle: The Mountaineers, 1969 reprint. - 309 p. : ill. , index.
A book of second aid for persons involved in accidents away from medical help. Starts where first
aid finishes, and a must for any group going on long
trips to isolated areas. Ed.

1088 WILKINSON, Thomas
Tours of the British mountains: with the descrip-
tive poems of Lowther and Emont Vales/ by Thomas
Wilkinson. - Taylor & Hessey, 1824. - 320 p.

1089 WILLEY, B. G.
History of the White Mountains/ by B. G. Willey.
Rev. by Frederick Thompson.

1090 _____.
Incidents in White Mountain history/ by B. G.
Willey.

1091 WILLIAMS, Cicely
Women on the rope: the feminine share in moun-

tain adventure/ by C. Williams. - London: Allen &
Unwin, 1973. - 240 p. : ill. , ports. , 23 cm. , bibl.

1092   .
          Zermatt saga/ by Cicely Williams, foreword by
Sir Arnold Lunn. - London: George Allen & Unwin,
1964. - 197 p. : ill. , 21 1/2 cm.

WILLIAMS, Joe see MONKHOUSE, Frank (636)

1093   WILLIAMS, John Harvey
          The mountain that was "God" ... which the Indians
named "Tacoma," but which is officially called "Rainier"/ by J. H. Williams. - New York: Putnam, 1911. -
142 p. : ill.

1094   WILLS, Sir Alfred
          "The Eagle's Nest" in the Valley of Sixt: a sum-
mer home among the Alps, together with some excursions among the Great Glaciers/ London: 1860.
          "Well written and skilful record of the author's ex-
periences, but does not compare with his previous
Wanderings [1095]. " RHB.

1095   .
          Wanderings among the high Alps/ by Sir Alfred
Wills. - 2nd ed. - Oxford: Blackwell, 1937. - 235 p.
(Blackwell's mountaineering library, no. 3)
          First pub. 1856. "Possibly the first English re-
cord of a number of climbs purely for pleasure with
no ulterior scientific motive ... Chamonix, Saas and
Zermatt...." NBL.

1096   WILSON, Andrew
          The abode of snow: observations on a journey
from Chinese Tibet to the Indian Caucasus, through
the upper valleys of the Himalaya/ by A. Wilson. -
Edinburgh and London: 1876.

1097   .
          A summer ramble in the Himalayas: with sport-
ing adventure in the Vale of Cashmere/ ed. by Mountaineer, with an intro. by J. Hume. - London: Hurst
and Blackett, 1860. - 358 p. : plates.

1098   WILSON, Claude
          An epitome of fifty years' climbing/ by Claude

Wilson. : privately printed, 1933. - 119 p.

1099 _____ .
Mountaineering/ by Claude Wilson; with illus. by
E. Carr. - London: Methuen, 1893. - 208 p.

1100 WILSON, Edward Livingston
Mountain climbing/ by E. L. Wilson, and others. -
London: Out of the door Library, 1897, 1911. 358 p.

1101 WILSON, Henry Schutz
Alpine ascents and adventures: or rock and snow
sketches ... with two illustrations by M. Stone ... and
E. Whymper/ by H. S. Wilson. - London: Sampson
Low, 1878. - xi, 319 p. : ill.

1102 WILSON, James Gilbert
Aorangi: the story of Mount Cook/ by J. G. Gilbert. - Christchurch, N. Z. : Whitcombe & Tombs,
1968. - 253 p. : ill. , maps, ports.
A history of the mountain from the beginning to
the present day. Its conquests and most interesting
climbs by both men and women plus photographs are
of interest to persons intending to visit New Zealand.
Ed.

1103 WILSON, John Douglas Bruce
The southern highlands/ by John Douglas Bruce
Wilson; including an appendix on rock climbing in the
Arrochar District/ by B. H. Humble and J. B. Nim-
lin. - Scottish Mountaineering Club, 1949. - 204 p. :
plates, maps. (The Scottish Mountaineering Club guide)

WILSON, Ken see SOPER, Jack (909)

WILSON, Maurice see ROBERTS, Dennis (804)

1104 WINDHAM, William
An account of the glaciers or ice Alps of Savoy:
in two letters; one from an English gentlemen (W.
Windham, assisted by R. Price and B. Stillingfleet)
... the other from P. Martel, Engineer with a map
and two views (from drawings by R. Price and P.
Martel)/ by W. Windham and P. Martel. - London:
Royal Society, 1744.
"Scientific record ... of the first expedition to ob-
serve the Mer de Glace in the Mont Blanc range...."
NBL.

1105   WINTER SPORTS: Special articles/ by Sir Arnold
        Lunn, Humphrey H. Cobb, W. R. Rickmers, A. Gor-
        don Mitchell and others. - London: Athletic Press,
        1926. - 120 p. : plates.

1106   WOLF, Siegfried Helmut
            The magic of the Alps: a collection of the most
        beautiful photographs ever taken in the Alps with notes
        on the essential feature of alpine life/ comp. by S.
        H. Wolf and others; trans. from the German by Oskar
        Konstandt. - 80 p. : plates.

1107   WOOD, Robert L.
            Across the Olympic mountains: the Press expedi-
        tion, 1889-90/ Robert L. Wood. - Seattle: University
        of Washington Press, - 220 p. : ill. , maps.
            An account of six men, four dogs and two mules
        in a pioneering exploration of this region. Valuable
        for historical background to early American mountain-
        eering. Ed.

1108   WORKMAN, Fanny Bullock
            Ice bound heights of the Mustagh: an account of
        two seasons of pioneer exploration and high climbing in
        the Baltistan Himalaya/ by F. B. & William Hunter
        Workman. - London: Archibald Constable, 1908. -
        444 p. : 170 ill. , 2 maps, 23 cm.

1109   _____.
            In the ice world of the Himalayas, among the peaks
        and passes of Ladakh, Nubru, Suru and Battistan/ by
        F. B. Workman. - London: Fisher Unwin, 1900. -
        204 p. : maps, ill.

1110   _____.
            Peaks and glaciers of Nun Kun: a record of pio-
        neer-exploration and mountaineering in the Punjab
        Himalaya/ by F. B. & William Hunter Workman. -
        London: Constable 1909. - 204 p. : 92 ill. , map, 27 cm.

1111   _____.
            Two summers in the ice-wilds of the Eastern Kara-
        koram/ by F. B. & William Hunter Workman. - Lon-
        don: Fisher Unwin, 1917. - 296 p. : 141 plates, 3 maps.
            "A scientific expedition on glaciers and topography
        of the Eastern Karakoram with criticism and correc-
        tions of previous accounts with a strong feminist
        bias. " BRD.

1112 WORKMAN, William Hunter
The call of the snowy Hispar: a narrative of exploration and mountaineering on the Northern Frontier
of India ... with an appendix by Count Dr. Cesare
Calciati and Dr. Mathias Koncza/ by William Hunter
and Fanny Bullock Workman. - London: Constable,
1910. - xvi, 297 p. : 113 ill. , 2 maps.

1113 WRIGHT, Jeremiah Ernest Benjamin
Rockclimbing in Britain/ by J. E. B. Wright. -
Koyl, 1964. - 142 p. : plates, maps, diagrs. , bibl.
Professional advice on the best places to climb,
by the director of training of the Mountaineering Asso-
ciation. Ed.

1114 _____.
The technique of mountaineering: a handbook of
established methods/ by J. E. B. Wright; with drawings by W. J. Kidd. - London: Nicholas Kaye; under
the auspices of the Mountaineering Association, 1955. -
191 p. : ill. , 20 plates, maps, 20 1/2 cm.
See also MURRAY, William Hutchison (681);
BURNS, W. C. (149a)

1115 WYATT, Colin
Call of the mountains/ by Colin Wyatt. - London:
Thames & Hudson, 1952. - 95 p. : 75 plates.
"Combines skiing with mountaineering, written in
a fine sensitive style. Includes travels in Morocco,
Albania, Lapland, Canada, New Zealand Alps and Aus
tralia. Some awe inspiring plates. " BRD.

1116 WYMER, Norman George
Sir John Hunt/ by Norman George Wymer. - London: Oxford University Press, 1956. - 32 p. : front
(port.), ill. (Lives of great men and women, series 2,
no. 4)
A biography of a great mountaineer. Ed.

1117 YAKUSHI, Yoshimi
Catalogue of the Himalayan literature/ (by) Yoshimi
Yakushi. - Kyoto, Japan: The Author, 1972. - Limited ed. of 500. - 343 p.
A definitive study of the Himalayan region in two
parts; books in European languages, and books in
Japanese. Many entries are annotated. The subject
includes mountaineering as well as other aspects, such
as geography, studies of the people, etc. Ed.

156 / Mountaineering

1118 _____.
Gurla Himal: Japanese expedition to Nepal Himalaya, 1969/ ed. by Yoshimi Yakushi. - Tokyo: Toy-
ama, 1970. - 168 p. : 80 plates.
"80 plates with captions in English, text in Japanese. " Dawson's.

YAMADA, K. see SANUKI, M. (837)

1119 YANG, Ke-Hsien
The ascent of the Mustagh Ata/ by Yang Ke-
Hsien. - Peking: Foreign Languages Press, 1956. -
60 p. : ill. , map.
"Account of the Russo-Chinese expedition to Mustagh Ata in the Pamirs in 1956. They reached the
summit on July 31st. In August 1947, Shipton and
Tilman reached the summit plateau, but did not actual-
ly attain the highest point. " Yakushi.

YARD, R. S. see TOLL, Roger W. (997)

1120 YELD, George
Scrambles in the eastern Graians, 1878-1897/ by
George Yeld. - London: Fisher Unwin, 1900. - xx,
279 p. : ill. , map.

1121 YODA, T.
Ascent of Manaslu in photographs, 1952-56/ by
Tog T. Yoda. - New York: Tuttle, 1957.

1122 YORKSHIRE RAMBLERS' CLUB
Yorkshire Ramblers' Club library [catalogue]. -
Leeds: the Club, 1959. - 154 p.
A well set-out bibliography in geographical se-
quences of books presently held in the Leeds Public
Libraries. The author index is particularly useful. Ed.

1123 YOUNG, Bert Edward
Edward Whymper: alpinist of the heroic age. A
paper printed in the Popular Science Monthly, June
1913/ by Bert Edward Young. - Nashville, Tenn. :
Private circulation, 1914. - 9 p.

1124 YOUNG, Geoffrey Winthrop
Freedom/ by Geoffrey Winthrop Young. - London:
Smith, Elder, 1914. - viii, 148 p.
Poems.

1125

         _____ .
       The grace of forgetting/ by Geoffrey Winthrop
Young. - London: Country Life, 1953. - 352 p.:
plates, port.
       Autobiographical: the author's life from youth
until 1918. Ed.

1126

         _____ .
       The influence of mountains upon the development
of human intelligence/ by Geoffrey W. Young. - Glasgow: Jackson, 1957. - 30 p.
       (Glasgow University Publications)

1127

         _____ .
       Mountaincraft/ by Geoffrey Winthrop Young. - 7th
ed. - London: Methuen, 1954. - 603 p.: plates.
       First pub. 1920. "The classic on the fundamental
principles. " Alan Blackshaw. "394 pages of discussion
by the author, 63 pages on mountaineering on skis by
Sir Arnold Lunn, leaving 162 pages for eleven contri-
butors plus an index. " BRD.

1128

         _____ .
       Mountains with a difference/ by Geoffrey Winthrop
Young. - London: Eyre and Spottiswoode, 1951. -
281 p.: plates. (New Alpine Library)
       "Pre-1914 climbs--pioneering on Welsh rocks,
Irish and Scottish hills. Classical alpine routes including the Matterhorn and Grepon made with an artificial leg. " NBL.

1129

         _____ .
       On high hills: memories of the Alps/ by Geoffrey
Winthrop Young. - London: Methuen, 1927. - 368 p.:
24 ill.
       "Chronicles ascents from 1900 to 1914 ... new
routes ... with or without guides, particularly on the
great south face of Mont Blanc. " NBL.

1130

         _____ .
       The roof-climber's guide to Trinity [College]: con-
taining a practical description of all routes/ by Geoffrey
Winthrop Young. - Cambridge: W. P. Spaulding, 1899. -
34 p.: map, plates.

1131

         _____ .
       Snowden biography/ by G. W. Young, Geoffrey

Sutton and W. Noyce/ ed. by Wilfred Noyce. - London: Dent, 1957. - 194 p. : ill. , map.

1132 _____.
Wall and roof climbing/ by Geoffrey Winthrop Young. - London: 1905.

1133 YOUNG, Peter
Himalayan holiday: a trans-Himalayan diary, 1939/ by Peter Young. - London: Jenkins, 1945. - 108 p. : ill.

1134 YOUNGHUSBAND, Sir Francis Edward
Epic of Mt. Everest/ by Sir Francis Younghusband. - London: Edward Arnold, 1926. - 319 p. : ill.

1135 _____.
Everest: the challenge/ by Sir Francis Younghusband. - London: Nelson, 1936. - 243 p. : ill. , plates, maps, 24 cm.
"For the general public, an interesting account of the major expeditions of both the Germans and the British. The second part consists of philosophical reflections on the beauties of mountain climbing. " BRD.

1136 _____.
The heart of a continent: travels in Manchuria, the Gobi desert, the Himalayas, the Pamirs and Chitral, 1884-1894/ by Sir Francis Younghusband. - 2nd ed. - London: Murray, 1896. - 409 p. : ill.

1137 _____.
The light of experience: a review of some men and events of my time/ by Sir Francis Younghusband. - London: Constable, 1927. - 305 p.

1138 _____.
Wonders of the Himalayas/ by Sir Francis Younghusband. - London: Murray, 1924. - 210 p. : ill.
See also SAMUEL, Herbert L. (835)

1139 ZERMATTEN, Maurice
Mountains/ by M. Zermatten; mountaineering schools in Switzerland/ by Michael Vaucher; Woodcuts by Bruno Gentinetta, English version by Reginald Augustus Langford. - Zurich: Swiss National Tourist Office, 1967. - 36 p. : ill.

1140   ZURBRIGGEN, Mattias
       From the Alps to the Andes: being the autobio-
graphy of a mountain guide / by Mattias Zurbriggen,
translated by M. A. Vialls. - London: Fisher Unwin,
1899. - xvi, 269 p. : ill.
       "Zurbriggen climbed with Sir Martin Conway, Lt.
Col. C. Bruce, E. A. Fitzgerald, Fanny Bullock
Workman, among others. " Dawson's.

1141   ZURCHER, Frederic
       Mountain adventures in the various countries of the
world: selected from the narratives of celebrated
travellers / by F. Zurcher and Elie Margolle. - London: 1869. -   p. : 37 ill.

The craft of climbing 681
Crag and hound in Lakeland 82
Crag glacier and avalanche 238
The Cullin of Skye 461

D

Darjeeling at glance 56
A day and a night on the Aiguille du Dru 686
Day in, day out 526
The day the rope broke 183
Days of fresh air 23
Deborah 802
The delectable mountains 151
Dent Blanche 539
The descent of the Brenva face of Mont Blanc 540
A dictionary of mountaineering 207
Direttissima 366
A discourse on the attraction of mountains 766
Doctor on Everest 922
The Dolomite mountains 362
Dolomite strongholds 242
The Dolomites 178, 400, 622
Don Whillans 1071
The Drakensberg National Park 910

E

The Eagles' Nest in the valley of Sixt 1094
The early alpine guides 184
The Early American mountaineers 35
The early mountaineers 386
Early travellers of the Alps 247
East of Everest 433
East of Katmandu 1058
Easter climbs of the British Alpine Club 404
Eastern Alps 41
Eastern crags 270
An eccentric in the Alps 185
Edward W. D. Holway 729
Edward Whymper 892, 1123
Egmont 839
Eiger direct 366

Elementary mountaineering 661
The enchanted mountains 310
Encyclopaedic dictionary of mountaineering 231
English lakes 733
An English mountaineer 283
The English outcrops 1032
The Englishman in the Alps 560
Epic of Mt. Everest 1134
The epics of Everest 1082
Episodes in a varied life 217
Episodes of two seasons 541
An epitome of fifty years climbing 1098
Equipment for mountain climbing and camping 86
Equipment for mountaineering 607
Equipment for mountaineers 20, 251
Everest 645, 831
Everest: a guide to the climb 823
The Everest adventure 255
Everest climbed 854
Everest diary 573
Everest is climbed 706
Everest: is it conquered? 372
The Everest-Lhotse adventure 287
Everest 1952 813
Everest 1933 832
Everest: South Face 100a
Everest: the challenge 1135
Everest: the Swiss Everest expedition 957
Everest--West Ridge 450
The everlasting hills 1045
Everywhere 515
Expeditions on the glaciers 64
Exploration of Mount Kina Balu 1074
Exploration of the Caucasus 344
Exploring the Himalayas 267
Extracts from my journal 145
Eye on Everest 296

F

Fellcraft 470a
The fellwalker 1042

M

The magic of the Alps 1106
Makalu, 8470 metres 336
The making of a mountaineer 324
Mallory of Everest 944
Man of action, man of spirit 835
Man of Everest 040, 968
Man on the Matterhorn 1078
Manaslu, 1954-6 485
Manchester made them 176
Manual of American mountain-eering 426
Manual of ski mountaineering 123
Marching wind 180
Masherbrum, 1938 127
The Matterhorn 792
Matterhorn centenary 561
Matterhorn man 1033
Mazama 601
Medicine for mountaineering 1087
Memoirs of a mountaineer 170
Memories of mountains and men 405
Memory to memory 562
Men against Everest 593a
Men against the clouds 146
Men and the Matterhorn 785
Men and mountaineering 945
Men aspiring 764
Men, books and mountains 923
Men, women and mountains 844
Mick Bowie 107
The Midlands Hindu Kush Expedition 848
Minus one hundred and forty-eight degrees 241
Minus three 594
Mischief in Greenland 989
Mischief in Patagonia 990
Mittel Switzerland 28
The Moated mountain 946
Modern mountaineering 6, 947
Moments of being 383a
Mt. Blanc 280, 291, 996
Mont Blanc and the Aiguilles 623

Mont Blanc and the seven valleys 350
Mont Blanc by the Brenva 543
Mont Blanc sideshow 982
Mont Blanc to Everest 786
Moors, crags and caves of the high peak 44
More than mountains 480
Mount Cook Alpine Region 430a
Mount Cook and its surrounding glaciers 590
Mount Everest 31, 393 459
The Mount Everest expeditions of 1921, 1922 653
Mount Everest: 1938 991
The Mount Everest Reconnaissance expedition, 1951 861
Mount Foraker 128
Mt. Garibaldi Park 676
Mt. McKinley 642
Mount McKinley and mountain climbers' proofs 50
Mt. Rainier 606
The Mountain 610, 1037
Mountain adventure at home and abroad 7
Mountain adventures 556
Mountain adventures in various parts of the world 420
Mountain adventures in the various countries of the world 1141
A mountain and a man 171
Mountain ascents in Westmoreland and Cumberland 65
Mountain called Nun Kun 752
The mountain challenge 906
Mountain climbing 204, 334, 1100
The mountain code 056
Mountain conquest 449
Mountain days in the highlands and Alps 1043
Mountain days near home 825
Mountain essays by famous climbers 108
Mountain exploration 49
Mountain fever 395
Mountain holidays 662

A selected list on mountaineering 817
Selected list of books on mountaineering 488
A selection of some 900 British and Irish mountaintops 262
Seven years in Tibet 408
The shameless diary of an explorer 274
Shelf catalogue of the Lloyd collection of Alpine books 546
A short account of Mont Blanc 867
A short history of lakeland climbing 495
A short manual of mountaineering training 149a
A short walk in the Hindu Kush 694
Siberia 1008
Siege of Nanga Parbat 74
Simen 600
Sir Edmund Hillary 505
Sir John Hunt 1116
Sir John Hunt's diary 464
Six great mountaineers 190
Six letters relating to travel, 1865-69 363
Skiing for beginners and mountaineers 797
The sky was his limit 587
Snow camping and mountaineering 821
Snow commando 62
Snow on the Equator 993
Snow sentinels of the Pacific Northwest 419
Snowden biography 1131
Snowden south 493
Some Cumbrian climbs and equipment 398
Some mountain expeditions of the Parkers 309
Some mountain views 751
Some notes on Mountaineering in the high Atlas 355a
Some Oberland climbs 782
Some peaks 721
Some shorter climbs in Derbyshire and elsewhere 524
Son of the mountains 512

Songs of the cragsmen 68
Songs of the mountaineers 441
South Col. 709
The southern highlands 1103
Southern mountaineers 725
Space below my feet 631
Specifications for climbers helmets 117a
Specifications for mountaineering ropes 117
The spell of the mountains 399
The spirit of the hills 902
The spirit of the Matterhorn 265
Spitzbergen 714
The splendid hills 191
Sport and travel in the highlands of Tibet 417
Sport in the Alps, past and present 389
Springs of adventure 710
Stalks in the Himalayas 921
Standard encyclopaedia of the world's mountains 469
Starlight and storm 789
Stefano: we shall come tomorrow 870
Stories of alpine adventure 678
The story of alpine climbing 387
The story of Annapurna 496
The story of Everest 684, 697
The story of Mont Blanc 877
The story of mountains 517
Straight up 1024
Strategy and tactics in mountain ranges 584
The structure of the Alps 202
Stubai Alps 805
A study of the literature of mountains and of mountain climbing written in English 70
Summer holidays in the Alps 279
Summer months in the Alps 439
A summer ramble in the Himalayas 1097

With axe and rope in the New
    Zealand Alps 588
With sack and stock in Alaska
    120
With Whymper in the Alps
    1050
A woman's reach 646
Women on the rope 1091
Wonders of Darjeeling and Sik-
    kim Himalaya 59
Wonders of the Himalayas
    1138
The world at their feet 967
World atlas of mountaineering
    713

Y

Yorkshire Ramblers' Club Li-
    brary 1122
The Yosemite 668
The young mountaineer 1036
Your rope 116
You're standing on my fingers
    537

Z

Zermatt and district 209
Zermatt and its valleys 371
Zermatt and the Valois 572
Zermatt saga 1092
Zigzagging among Dolomites
    1006

SUBJECT INDEX

AFRICA 148, 158, 281, 490,
500, 611, 691, 811, 910,
911, 962, 993, 1003
ALPS (Europe) 7, 12, 15b,
18, 41, 48, 52, 80, 94, 99,
106, 114, 118, 119, 149,
181, 202, 205, 208, 212,
223, 245, 279, 292, 324,
331, 332, 345, 356, 389,
439, 447, 471, 502, 506,
527, 528, 555, 613, 615,
616, 641, 650, 671, 675,
680a, 702, 703, 745, 750,
758, 781, 782, 795, 805,
809, 837, 844, 846, 866,
881, 884, 908, 924, 935,
964, 970, 983, 1009, 1012,
1015, 1016, 1025, 1043,
1050, 1051, 1054, 1069,
1079, 1094, 1095, 1101,
1104, 1128, 1129, 1140.
see also specific references
under individual mountains,
e. g. MATTERHORN or
MONT BLANC
AMERICA (U. S. A.) 22, 103,
120, 167, 234, 304, 352,
413, 418, 498, 531, 617,
660, 667, 810, 1040
ANDES (South America) 38,
109, 194, 211, 215, 219,
230, 286, 316, 328, 501,
508, 521, 612, 747, 750,
871, 990, 1022, 1044, 1080,
1140
ANNAPURNA 100, 376, 391,
429, 496, 509, 970
AUSTRALIA 38, 303, 628,
959, 1029, 1115

BIBLIOGRAPHY 84, 111, 157,
199, 248, 305, 306, 318,

488, 538, 546, 637, 638,
760, 769, 798, 817, 824,
880, 1117, 1122
BIOGRAPHY--Collections 27,
85, 172, 184, 190, 193,
235, 247, 248, 264, 278,
293, 386, 402, 672, 708,
725, 844, 888, 920, 937,
950, 967, 1030, 1137.
see also individual bio-
graphies and autobiographies
in the main sequence
BRITISH COLUMBIA 676,
677, 978

CAUCASUS 140, 276, 326,
344, 348, 355a, 411, 422,
467, 674, 675, 1095

DENT BLANCHE 539, 544
DHAULAGIRI 288, 391
DOLOMITES 178, 242, 285,
345, 362, 400, 457, 622,
793, 869, 935, 1005, 1034

EIGER (Eigerwand) 101, 256,
366, 408, 432, 604, 718,
870, 1024, 1034
EQUIPMENT 20, 86, 116,
117, 117a, 163, 177, 204,
251, 284a, 308, 398, 577,
607, 954, 964a, 1068
EVEREST see MOUNT EV-
EREST

GREAT BRITAIN (General) 2,
3, 7, 17, 40, 43, 62a, 65,
79, 80, 81, 92, 95, 111,
141, 155, 160, 175, 188,
195, 262, 492, 495, 524,
682, 685, 771, 773, 774,
775, 882, 903, 929, 1032,

178